CHURCH REFUGEES

Sociologists reveal why people are DONE with church but not their faith

Loveland, CO

Group
Real. Bold. Love.

JOSH PACKARD, PH.D. and ASHLEIGH HOPE

CHURCH REFUGEES
Sociologists Reveal Why People Are Done
With Church but Not Their Faith

Credits
Senior Editor: Candace McMahan
Copy Editor: Christy Fagerlin
Cover Art Director: Darrin Stoll
Interior: Andy Towler

Library of Congress Cataloging-in-Publication Data

Packard, Josh.
  Church refugees : sociologists reveal why people are done with church but not their faith / Josh Packard, Ph.D. and Ashleigh Hope. -- First American hardcover.
      pages cm
  ISBN 978-1-4707-2791-8 (hardcover) -- ISBN 978-1-4707-2592-1 (softcover)
  1. Ex-church members. I. Hope, Ashleigh, 1993- II. Title.
  BV4921.3.P33 2015
  262--dc23

                              2015005788

ISBN 978-1-4707-2791-8

10 9 8 7 6 5 4 3 2 1   24 23 22 21 20 19 18 17 16 15

Printed in the United States of America.

TABLE OF CONTENTS

ACKNOWLEDGMENTS

As academics, we don't often get to write for a general audience, but I was cheered on by my fantastic colleagues at the University of Northern Colorado and friends and mentors Dr. Richard Pitt at Vanderbilt University and Dr. George Sanders at Oakland University. My wife, Megan, who has never read a word of anything I've written, never needs to, as far as I'm concerned. Her influence is felt throughout this project. I couldn't ask for a better partner in life, and our son couldn't ask for a better mother.

I couldn't have written this book without Ashleigh Hope. Indeed, this project may very well have sat on my shelf for many more years if she hadn't come along and asked for some work to do. She's a once-in-a-lifetime student whom I'm proud to have as a colleague. There are, no doubt, more great things to come from her.

—Josh Packard

I would like to thank my Savior for making all things new and continuing the good works he's begun within me. Additionally, I'm grateful for my beloved husband, Kyle, for encouraging me in this research and all others. His support and insight have been invaluable.

—Ashleigh Hope

We would both like to express our gratitude for the amazing team at Group Publishing. They've been invaluable. Thom Schultz's willingness to meet with us following an unsolicited email is behavior not normally associated with presidents of large companies. He and his wife, Joani, have championed this project from the beginning. The concept of the refugee as a metaphor first came up in conversations with Amy Nappa, and the writing and publishing process was demystified and smoothed out by an extraordinary group of professionals at Group Publishing consisting of Craig Cable, Mikal Keefer, Becky Hodges, and Candace McMahan, among others.

Finally, we're both deeply indebted to all who shared their stories for this research. Their honesty and vulnerability made this book possible.

CHURCH REFUGEES

FOREWORD

A few years ago, in the course of collecting data for a different project, I (Josh) had the occasion to talk with some church planters and ministry resource leaders over lunch. In some way or another, they all wanted to know why so many people were leaving the church. Finally, one relatively new pastor asked the group, "So what's different about this era that so many people are leaving the church? What happened?"

As I began to formulate some kind of answer based on all of my recently completed graduate schooling in sociology, Jessica, a woman who had been working in ministry-resource publication for over two decades, spoke up: "Nothing. People have always been leaving the church. It's just that now they're not coming back. That's the real issue. We're doing things that drive people away from the church. *We're* the problem. We've dechurched them. They're done with us."

Jessica's words hung over the table for a few seconds that felt like hours before I broke the uneasy silence by asking, "So, what do you all think? Is Jessica right? Of the people you know who've left, do you think they're coming back? Do you know why they left?"

One by one, they all revealed that, indeed, they didn't think any of the people who had left their congregations would be coming back with the exception of a general and vague hope that young people going off to college would eventually return. Instead, they related story after story of people who had left their congregations after prolonged struggle, searching, and sometimes incredibly harmful and divisive experiences.

As they recounted the reasons people had given them for leaving their churches, I heard about pastors behaving poorly; churches focused so much on buildings and infrastructure that they neglected the outside world; unwanted and distracting political stances; perceived persecution over issues of gender and sexuality; hypocrisy; and many, many stories about judgment.

They weren't recounting the transgressions of an anonymous church down the street or of friends who pastor congregations in other towns. These were stories that pastors and other church leaders were telling about their own congregations. These were things that happened on their watch, despite their best intentions. It remains, several years later, among the most revealing moments I've ever encountered in my research.

Aside from being heartbroken to hear these stories of hurt, disillusionment, and bitterness at the hands of trusted people in a trusted institution, I was intrigued sociologically. What, for example, did Jessica mean by "dechurched"? Who are these people—the "Dones"—and how do they make the decision to leave the church? Does their leaving accompany a loss of faith in God or a change in religious affiliation? Furthermore, how can we understand the institutional forces that seemingly work to compel poor behavior from a group of well-meaning pastors working in organizations with the explicit mission to be loving, just, and compassionate?

As so often happens in the course of research, these questions weren't central to the project I was working on at the time, and so I filed them away, but they were never far from my mind. As I began teaching Sociology of Religion courses on a regular basis, I heard more and more stories similar to the ones those religious leaders had told me. Typically, students would recount their negative experiences with organized religion after class or during office hours as we worked to apply a particular theory or reconcile some empirical evidence we'd been reading with our own personal experiences.

Again and again, I returned to this concept of the dechurched and the Dones, and increasingly, my own students were using it to describe their experiences. In the midst of these thoughts, my research assistant, Ashleigh Hope, approached me and said, "We should really look into this. Why is church so bad to some people? And more important sociologically, what happens to our society if this central institution continues to drive people away?"

This book was born out of those questions. Primarily, we're interested in understanding precisely what it means to be "done" with organized religion, uncovering its effect on the institution of religion, beginning to assess what social forces are driving this trend, and what it means for the future of such a historically important institution in the United States.

More personally, we have a heart for the church and want it to succeed, though we aren't particularly sympathetic to any specific form of church, institutional or otherwise.

So this book is best understood as an amalgamation of those two impulses. It's an accounting of the dechurched phenomenon from sociologists who apply our understanding of social theory to explain why people are increasingly done with organized religion, what it means for churches across this country, and what can be done about it.

A NOTE ABOUT THE RESEARCH

THE PROJECT'S BIRTH

This project, like all good social science, started with a question. Quite simply, we kept hearing stories of people who were disengaging with church but not with God. We wanted to know why this was happening and what the process of disengagement looked like.

Of course, we had lots of hypotheses when we started out. For a while we thought maybe the answer had something to do with generations. We kept hearing about the rise of the "Nones" (those who claim no religious affiliation) and thought that this might be a part of that story, which is very much a generational phenomenon.

We read through our sociology of religion literature and were also working with a hypothesis that the rise of the dechurched, the people we would come to call the Dones, was somehow connected to the dominance of conservative Christian theology. We thought maybe the dechurched were the more theologically liberal who couldn't find a home in the church.

We also had good reason to believe that the poor behavior of pastors and others church leaders (clergy molesting children, youth directors embezzling funds, pastors cheating on spouses, and so on) was exposing a level of moral corruption that was driving people away.

As it turns out, none of these hypotheses was correct. Instead, it became clear to us that the story of the dechurched was a story of modern religious organizations and institutions stifling people's ability to engage with each other and their communities.

OUR METHODS

Many people have inquired about our research methods. As researchers, we love the fact that people are consuming data and information critically, and we invite these conversations and affirm the impulse to be critical consumers. In the following pages, we outline our general approach and defend some of our more important choices. If you find yourself with additional questions, we are more than happy to explain further. You may reach us at www.dechurched.net or via our Twitter account, @DechurchAmerica or at josh.packard@unco.edu.

The research for this book was conducted between January 2013 and July 2014. The research design, protocol, and instruments were crafted to the highest academic standards and rigor and were passed through the Institutional Review Board at the University of Northern Colorado. In accordance with those standards, the identifying details of the individuals, congregations, and places in this book have been altered. While demographic data such as region, age, and gender remain unchanged, pseudonyms have been assigned to each person in the study.

One of the questions we're frequently asked is about our statistics, or the lack thereof. People are used to seeing numbers to explain the world around us. But numbers tell us very little, if anything, about people's experiences, interpretations, and processes. As we honed our research questions, it became clear that a survey that would generate numbers and statistics would be virtually impossible for two primary reasons.

First, the dechurched, by their nature, don't gather together regularly or belong to the same kinds of organizations. It would make the things necessary for a scientifically valid survey, such as random sampling, unfeasible without first understanding the basic characteristics of the group.

Second, based on the wildly varied hypotheses we came up with, it was evident that we couldn't even begin to construct survey questions that would accurately account for all of the potential answers someone might give to any one question. We were worried that an attempt to squeeze people into selecting one of five or six options we provided wouldn't provide an accurate understanding of what it means to leave the church, why people leave, or how the process happens. For these reasons, then, we abandoned the idea of taking a quantitative approach and turned to qualitative methods as the appropriate way to get answers to our questions.

Future work in this area would do well to build on the findings presented here in pursuit of quantifiable evidence that can give full scope to this large and rapidly growing group of Christians.

QUALITATIVE RESEARCH

Qualitative research is particularly good for findings that require stories and conversations from participants. From the researcher, it requires discipline, forethought, and creativity to guide interviews in a way that stays on track with the research question without leading participants into answers.

We're thankful for the solid methodological foundations provided by sociological researchers working throughout the last century to hone in on sets of best practices and guidelines for gathering rigorous empirical data that can help us better understand social phenomena.

Additionally, we're thankful for the advent of modern qualitative analysis software that allowed us to analyze each of the interviews for key themes and evaluate all of the evidence together. In a project of this size, with over 1,000 pages of transcriptions, we simply couldn't have kept it all straight otherwise.

Each word and sentence of every interview was coded and analyzed according to classic principles in qualitative data analysis. The entire project was approved by the University of Northern Colorado Institutional Review Board and supported by several research grants. Results have been presented at several academic conferences, and a manuscript for an article in the academic Journal for the Scientific Study of Religion is in progress. In other words, while this particular manuscript has not been peer-reviewed, the data collection and analysis procedures and many of the results presented in these pages have held up to rigorous scientific review, and we're fully confident in the validity of the empirical research presented here.

As with any research, however, there are limits to our findings. First, and most important, this research gives no indication of the scope of the dechurched phenomenon. In other words, nothing in these pages can provide an indication of how many dechurched exist in the world, or in the United States.

But we can be confident in the key themes and processes identified in the following chapters. Our confidence is based on two primary factors. First, the remarkable consistency in our data and the diversity of our sample provide assurance that the themes we see in the data are not simply a coincidence.

Second, qualitative research generally relies on the principle of saturation when deciding how much data to collect. That is, when researchers reach the point where they keep seeing or hearing the same things again and again, that's a good sign that there is consistency and thus a general social pattern. However, we continued to collect data well past the point of saturation because we simply couldn't believe how consistently the data contradicted our initial hypotheses.

In short, if we were going to tell a counterintuitive story about the dechurched, we wanted to make sure we were right. As the theme of the stifling institutional structure emerged and the other hypotheses fell by the wayside, we decided we had to collect more data and actually began looking for cases to contradict this emerging pattern. Alas, the contradictory case virtually never emerged and certainly not in a way that would suggest an alternative pattern.

WHO ARE THE RESPONDENTS?

A number of people have also asked specifically about our sample and how we found and recruited participants. The issue of sampling qualitative research is somewhat more complicated than I think most people would expect, and our project is no exception.

First, it's important to understand how our sample was generated. We worked with the principles of snowball or chain-referral sampling. This relies on the idea that people who are dechurched are likely to come into contact with one another and share their stories with one another. At the end of each interview, we asked the participant to refer us to other people he or she knew who would fit the description of our research. Along the way, however, we were constantly checking our demographic information to make sure we weren't missing entire populations of people in ways that we thought would matter. For example, we didn't want a sample that contained no poor people because the literature in the sociology of religion has long shown that religious habits vary greatly by income and social class.

In order to achieve a diverse sample, we started our snowballs in places where we could expect to reach different audiences. Key points in our recruitment came when Thom Schultz, the president of Group Publishing, invited people to visit our website, www.dechurched.net, through a link on his Facebook page. Around that same time, we reached out to other pastors and people in ministry to help spread the word. Many of our early interviews came from those sources. Additionally, we both have long histories in the church and leveraged those contacts for some key early interviews that allowed us to test out some early hypotheses and ideas. Finally, as word about the project spread, we generated interest through our own Twitter, @DechurchAmerica, and sustained interviews for over 18 months resulting in nearly 100 in-depth interviews at the time of writing.

The result is a sample that is diverse geographically, socioeconomically (average household income is $55,745), generationally (average age is 40 years old with a spread from 18 to 84 years old), and with regard to gender (56 percent female), but is racially homogenous. Our respondents are nearly all white (92 percent). However, we don't see anything in the data to contradict our conclusion that this is an issue of resources, not of race.

The story that emerged from the data is that people with access to alternative ways of reaching their goals of community and social engagement are opting out of church. In our society, this is typically white people for issues of social class, not because of heritage, tradition, or ethnicity. White people in the U.S. have much greater access to social institutions and systems of power, so when they leave the church, they can find other ways of getting things done. Also, white people generally have much more social and cultural capital than other groups, making it more possible for them to realize their goals without a supporting institution.

The one caveat to this is probably with regard to African-Americans. Because of longstanding issues surrounding their forced migration, the African-American assimilation process has been uneven at best, and the church has come to play a defining role for many African-American communities as a source of identity. In this sense, then, the church plays a somewhat different role and is subject to different organizational dynamics. It would be impossible to speculate about how far the findings presented here would extend into the African-American church in America. Indeed, a full-scale study of this population is certainly warranted.

Additionally, we administered a validated scale of religious fundamentalism as early research into this area indicated that the nature of people's religious beliefs might impact their decision-making process in terms of attendance at religious events. The results of our analysis of this scale showed no distinct patterns. Not only did a roughly equal number of people fall at all points on the scale, but their answers on the scale were not predictive of their persistence in church or their pathways out of church.

If Ashleigh and I could communicate one thing about the demographics of the Dones, it would be that this is an issue of talents and energy, not of numbers. While we have strong suspicions about the rising numbers of Dones, this is, ultimately, not a story of numbers. It's a story of what happens when an organization invests in training and discipling scores of people and yet does very little to retain them or reengage them when they leave.

CHAPTER 1: THE DECHURCHED AS RELIGIOUS REFUGEES

WHO ARE THE DECHURCHED?

This is a book about leaving the church. For years now, in the social sciences, we've had a pretty good grasp of the social forces that pattern people's religious lives. Clergy and academics alike are familiar with the more common patterns. Kids grow up in religious homes, go off to college, stop attending church regularly, but come back when they have their own children because of a belief that their kids should have some of the same religious upbringing. A woman moves to a new city because of a job promotion, never finds a church, and eventually stops looking. A man goes through a divorce and stops going to church to avoid his ex-wife.

On top of all of these patterns are the larger social forces that influence any given generation of churchgoers. The televangelist and clergy sex-abuse scandals of the 1980s influenced an entire decade of church attendance figures. Our changing economy over the last 50 years to include increasingly more shift labor makes regular Sunday morning attendance a challenge for many. The increasing diversity of our country makes it harder for one social group to lay claim to a particular day of the week where all other activity stops. When our kids' soccer games are scheduled for Sunday mornings, and work retreats, travel, and conferences extend through the weekend, regular church involvement becomes increasingly difficult.

Still, what most of these scenarios have in common is that they're tales of unintentional leaving. Other life circumstances and events got in the way of continued church attendance. If life had remained the same—if the child hadn't gone away to college, if the woman hadn't been promoted, if the man hadn't gotten divorced—they would all likely have remained in church. But this book isn't about them.

This book is about a wholly different kind of churchgoer. It's about people who make explicit and intentional decisions to leave the church and organized religion. We call these people the dechurched or the Dones: They're done with church. They're tired and fed up with church. They're dissatisfied with the structure, social message, and politics of the institutional church, and they've decided they and their spiritual lives are better off lived outside of organized religion. As one of our respondents put it, "I guess the church just sort of churched the church out of me."

> ## "I guess the church just sort of churched the church out of me."

THE STRUGGLE TO LEAVE

The dechurched typically struggle with the decision to leave for a long time. Some put up with spiritual abuse on a regular and repeated basis before finally leaving, and many are never fully comfortable with leaving even if they're sure that their decision to leave is the right one. Many, in fact, see leaving the church as the only way to save their faith.

In August 2013, Micah J. Murray, a popular religious blogger, expressed exactly these sentiments in his blog post "Why We Left the Church (Our Stories)":

"Don't say that we left because we didn't want to follow Jesus, or because we're too consumeristic, or too selfish, or too sinful. The self-righteous assumptions and finger-pointing are a kick in the ribs to those already paralyzed by fear and aching doubt. Please don't do that."

Mr. Murray's comments, which came after sharing numerous stories of people opting out of organized religion, sum up the central tensions and struggles of the dechurched. In short, leaving church is never an easy decision. You won't encounter a single story in this book of someone walking away from church on a whim or because of one bad experience. You won't hear that story because *we* didn't hear that story. If those stories exist, they're a small minority of experiences relative to the much more common tale of struggle and soul-searching over a prolonged period of time that typically precedes a decision to disengage with organized religion.

Churches are an institution that people identify with heavily in the United States. Even if trends in church attendance suggest a general decline in recent years, it remains a place of home and a central organizing identity for millions of Americans. For attendees, church serves some combination of spiritual, social, and civic needs. At its best, church organizes people to do things together that they couldn't do alone. Leaving such a place, then, often means giving up social connections, activity groups, and—perhaps most important—taking on a certain amount of spiritual guilt. Nobody enthusiastically walks away from those things or eagerly embraces feelings of guilt and shame.

> **Nobody enthusiastically walks away from those things or eagerly embraces feelings of guilt and shame.**

With this struggle as a backdrop, we'll delve into the stories and the patterns behind those individual experiences in an effort to provide a more nearly complete picture of why people would choose to leave the church and how those decisions are made. Such decisions are always personal, but there are common threads running through them.

REFUGEES

Refugees are people who've been forced from their homes—where they'd prefer to stay—for fear of persecution. That, in a nutshell, describes the dechurched. They feel they've been forced to leave a place they consider home because they feel a kind of spiritual persecution and it would be dangerous, spiritually, for them to remain. They tell stories of frustration, humiliation, judgment, embarrassment, and fear that caused them to leave the church. They remark time and again that they worked diligently for reform within the church but felt the church was exclusively focused on its own survival and resistant to change. If they stayed, they would risk further estrangement from their spiritual selves, from God, and from a religion they still believe in.

When considering the refugee metaphor for the dechurched, it's important to consider other metaphors for people without a home that are similar but aren't quite right. For example, they aren't ex-patriots. The refugee is a reluctant leaver, packing up only as a last resort. They aren't relocating in search of political or economic opportunities. They aren't explorers or travelers, people on self-imposed journeys of discovery. Nor are they vacationers, taking a break for a time of relaxation or leisure. No, first and foremost and in every way, refugees desire to remain home. They've been forced to flee for reasons beyond their control. In fact, they often stay in their homes long past the point of danger, willing to put up with untold risks, holding out hope that peace will return to their homeland before they're forced to flee.

In this book, we take up the task of understanding the dechurched as church refugees. They're people who've made an explicit and intentional decision to leave organized religion. They didn't drift away casually. They didn't move to a new city for a job and never got into the groove of church in a new community. They didn't marry agnostic spouses and give up on convincing them. No, at some point, the dechurched decided, in a very intentional way, that they would be better off leaving the church altogether.

The church, they feel, is keeping them from God. According to them, the church, not God, is the problem, and they've stayed in the church long past the point that it ceased to be fulfilling or even sustaining.

The church, not God, is the problem.

Furthermore, they flee the church not because they hate the church. They have, in fact, worked tirelessly on behalf of the church. They flee for their own spiritual safety, to reconnect with a God they feel has been made distant to them by the structure of religion as practiced in organizations.

SOCIETAL TRENDS

Before we can even begin to understand the motivations and decision-making processes of church refugees, we need to take a look at the broader religious landscape. In order to answer the question about what's different about our era, we must focus on those elements of our society that have affected people's ability to be engaged with organized religion.

The two most important macro-level trends are undoubtedly the loss of trust in social institutions in general and religious leaders in particular and the perception that religious institutions are no longer tied into the daily life of individuals as intimately as they once were. In other words, they're increasingly considered irrelevant.

Loss of Trust

It was just a generation or so ago that people expressed high levels of trust in religious leaders, and the church had a reputation as a force for good. Religious institutions in this country had been prominently involved in many of the human rights struggles from women's suffrage in the 19th century to the civil rights movement in the middle of the 20th century. Local and national religious groups have continually responded admirably to natural disasters and community tragedies. But people trusted religious institutions and leaders not just because they responded to their community needs in times of crisis, but because religious institutions were intimately and continually involved in their local communities. Religious leaders were involved in *doing* things, not simply *proclaiming* things.

In a matter of a few decades, however, that trust has severely eroded. Since 1977 the Gallup organization has regularly asked Americans to rate the honesty and ethical standards of many professions in the United States. In 2013 the clergy received its lowest score ever. The number of people who believe clergy has very high or high levels of honesty and ethical standards fell below 50 percent for the first time. But this was no blip on the radar screen. After peaking at a high of 67 percent in 1985, the decline has been a pretty steady march downward.

One of the people we interviewed for this project is a pastor whose congregation includes a number of formerly dechurched people. Bill is in his mid-30s and has been with his church since it started as a small group nearly a decade ago. He has no formal training or education as a pastor but has evolved into the role. Still, he rarely presents himself as a pastor, introducing himself instead with one of his other vocations. This is intentional, he says, because he found early on that identifying himself as a pastor actually worked against him in trying to gain trust and form relationships, especially with the dechurched people his church is attracting. During the course of our conversation, as if to underscore the findings of the Gallup poll, he said:

> It is 100 percent the case that my role as a pastor means that people are inclined to *distrust* me and my intentions. They're inclined from the beginning to think that I'm only interested in their money or telling them what to do. Their first thoughts are not as mine were when I was a child: "That man is a pastor. He must be a really good person who loves me." That implicit trust has been completely turned upside down. As a pastor and staff, we approach every day with the understanding that we need to focus on earning that trust back. It can never be assumed.

According to Bill, then, the loss of trust in religious institutions means that trust must be earned daily—and the work of reestablishing trust must be done long before the church does any of the work of telling people how to live.

Loss of Relevance

In her recent book *Sacred Stories, Spiritual Tribes: Finding Religion in Everyday Life*, sociologist Nancy Ammerman points out what our data confirm: People are as concerned about religion as ever and are finding religion in their daily lives. However, the trend across all age groups is to move away from church and religious institutions as the central organizing mechanism for this activity. The church is simply not seen as a relevant force in people's daily lives.

The church is simply not seen as a relevant force in people's daily lives.

Rather, people are much more likely to see the church as a kind of niche political institution that's ultimately not concerned with their day-to-day existence. They view the church as inwardly focused and consumed by the politics of its own survival.

What emerges from our data is a picture of a desire for community life, but not one that's centrally organized by a large institution. One could argue that in this sense the church is being caught up in the larger social shift away from institutionally organized life. While monoliths still dominate in nearly every area of social life, we increasingly see the development of thriving alternatives. While Walmart continues to be the dominant retailer in America, farmers' markets and the shop-local movement have seen significant gains in recent years. While the megachurch continues to be a force in American religion, the only other religious movement of note over the last decade in the United States has been the emerging church movement. There is, in other words, beginning to be a critical mass of people who are disinclined to organize their lives around a large, seemingly impenetrable organization. Some people, at least, are desiring a different experience in which they can still operate as a collective but also have an impact and shape their local environments.

This context is important because it has ramifications for how we understand the dechurched movement. As researchers in the sociology of religion, we don't suspect that the growing number of Dones represents a death blow for the church in America. There are simply not enough dechurched in terms of raw numbers to threaten the existence of institutionalized religion in this country. Additionally, the long history of religion in this country is filled with ups and downs and threats. The church in America is not the European model. The church in America is characterized by adaptation and innovation, not stagnation.

Revivals have consistently punctuated institutional religion in the United States. Take, for example the Great Awakenings that spanned the better part of America's history from the middle of the 1700s to the middle of the 1900s. As the country grew, expanded, and dealt with new challenges, religious institutions adapted and responded to emerging needs. More recently, the megachurch, which developed to meet the needs of a rapidly suburbanizing America, has dramatically altered the religious landscape. Rather than diminishing in the face of new challenges, the church in America creates new ways of engaging the populace.

However, the dechurched movement is a strong leading indicator of the loss of relevance and diminished importance of the church in our society. If the church can't manage to retain its most committed, devoted, and energetic followers, then it's destined to become a greatly diminished force in the social landscape, at least in the immediate future. If the church continues to run off faithful followers who are, by their nature or religious conviction, conciliatory, compromising, and nonjudgmental, then we will continue to see a church that's increasingly insular, alienating, and irrelevant.

In recent years we've seen other indicators of this trend from writers paying more attention to the broad implications of an increasingly isolated church. Books like David Kinnaman and Gabe Lyons' *unChristian*, Group Publishing's *Why Nobody Wants to Go to Church Anymore* and *Why Nobody Wants to Be Around Christians Anymore*, and Drew Dyck's *Generation Ex-Christian* along with more academic reports like the much heralded 2012 Pew report "'Nones' on the Rise" paint a picture of the church from both insiders and outsiders of an institution that's increasingly marginalized and losing some of its best and brightest, the very people the church is counting on to lead it into the future.

THE IMPORTANCE OF THE DECHURCHED

Why should we care about the dechurched? In many ways, what we found in the course of our study is that the dechurched may represent the proverbial canary in the coal mine. In 2011, the distinguished American sociologist Mark Chaves published *American Religion: Contemporary Trends*, but one of the titles kicked around for that book was *The Decline of American Religion* because, as he pointed out, while some societal trends have remained stable over the years and some have declined, no indicator of religious activity in the United States has increased. Drawing on data from the General Social Survey, he notes that in addition to other indicators which have remained stable, "the percentages of Americans who *know* that God exists (64 percent) say they've had a born-again experience (36 percent), and who pray several times a week (69 percent) have remained steady since the 1980s." When overall trends are so stable, why should we care as social scientists about a group of people who are leaving church? Well, as Chaves points out, there are some pretty important indicators that are declining. The much noted numbers about the decline in religious affiliation and decreasing attendance at worship services are particularly germane to this study. Chaves refers to these combinations of trends as a "softening" rather than portending outright doom for institutional expressions of religion.

George Barna and David Kinnaman, in their 2014 book *Churchless*, argue that the dechurched represent 33 percent of the American population. Furthermore, they claim that people characterized as dechurched are the fastest growing segment of the population. However, throughout their book they collapse the category of dechurched into the broader category of unchurched. We think this is unfortunate because the dechurched are a particular type of person distinct from the broader category of unchurched people. For their part, Barna and Kinnaman seem to recognize this as well. They admit that the issue of the dechurched is much more nuanced than the statistics they use to inform their book can convey. *Church Refugees* helps to fill in this gap by providing rigorous analysis along with qualitative data to understand the processes that people go through when they decide to leave the church, what they do when they leave, and what they ultimately want out of church.

However, Barna and Kinnaman do provide two specific pieces of data about the dechurched that are important to highlight.

First, the dechurched are not angry, in general. Leaving "simply reflects the firsthand experiences that led them to conclude churches are ill-equipped to support the flourishing life they hope for." Throughout this book you'll read stories of people who express something actually more damaging than anger toward the church. They aren't mad, for the most part. They're uninterested. They've looked at the data provided by their own lived experiences and decided that church is simply not where they can have the spiritual lives they want.

Second, and related, Barna and Kinnaman point out that "we must admit the possibility that our churches are somehow enabling many people to stall out on their journey toward deep, transformative faith." As we'll show, this is much more than a possibility. It's the reality that our respondents consistently expressed to us. Furthermore, we hope that by the end of this book, we'll be able to show that churches are not "somehow" enabling people. Rather, we will delineate the specific mechanisms that our respondents say stunt spiritual growth and institutional engagement.

What we note here, however, is that the dechurched not only contribute to the decline in religious affiliation and in worship attendance, but they may also be driving forces behind these trends. Almost without exception, our respondents were deeply involved and devoted to their churches up until the moment they left. They were integrated into leadership structures and church life, often organizing daily life around the church and attending some kind of church function two or more times a week. They're the kind of people who are drawn to activity.

Take Jeff, for example. He's 55 years old and recently retired, from both his job and his church, where he was active for three decades, serving in a variety of capacities, including worship leader and youth director. When we talked, he said he had to make a complete break with his church once he felt he could no longer have an impact there. He could not simply sit in the pew on Sunday and walk away. He told me, "It's just hard for me to be a passive worshipper. I've got to be in the mix. I'm a player. I've got to do things. That's how I understand my faith and how I understand God." Jeff's words summarize the theme that runs through the vast majority of our interviews. The dechurched are so active and involved because activity is central to their pursuit of God. They don't know any other way to be a Christian.

Additionally, not one person in our sample left the church after just one bad experience. They thought the church was important enough to keep trying and trying. In fact, in our sample the average number of churches attended prior to leaving is more than four, spanning a number of years, indicating an astonishing commitment to the institution. The dechurched wanted to make the institution work, and they often worked for years for reform from within. Although the dechurched are people who have walked away, I would never question their commitment. In fact, if it were possible to stack up the energies and activities of the dechurched, that tower may well reach higher than the energy and activity that remain inside the walls of the institution.

Clearly, the dechurched are outliers in the religious landscape. However, they're extremely important outliers. They're the ones who, prior to leaving, showed up at worship every week and tithed. They organized and participated in small-group activities, Bible studies, worship planning, church councils, elder teams, and a plethora of other activities and services that are the lifeblood of churches big and small. They were the keepers of organizational history and played a significant role in defining institutional identity.

They're the opposite of the free riders who consume church resources but contribute little. Indeed, their work and activity make it possible for a congregation to support the free riders who often make up the bulk of church attendees on a given Sunday. The idea that inside of every committed congregant exists a strong potential to become dechurched represents more than just the loss of one congregant; it represents the potential loss of the kind of activity necessary to keep the doors open.

The data for this book consist of nearly 100 in-depth interviews, and the general profile of our respondents supports the idea that the dechurched are highly valuable churchgoers.

Our respondents are generally financially stable, very likely to be married, and have substantially higher levels of education than the churchgoing population in general. The 2008 U.S. Religious Landscape Survey by Pew provides some interesting comparison data. While about 15 percent of the affiliated Christian population have a college degree, our *average* respondent has completed at least some graduate-level work, and an astonishing 87 percent are either currently enrolled in college or have completed an undergraduate degree. Furthermore, 77 percent of our sample over the age of 25 are married and report household incomes of around $65,000. Additionally, the vast majority have spent years in the church and in ministry positions.

These church refugees, then, aren't like the vast majority of churchgoers, and they aren't quite like the vast majority of the religiously unaffiliated. They are a stable, powerful, and important group of people.

Refugees are a significant concern for any society. Although the popular image of a refugee is of someone who is poor and powerless, living in substandard conditions, refugees also comprise those in a society who had the political, economic, and social capital to escape. And when they flee a society, they take all of those assets with them. The mass exodus of people from a country is rightly characterized in the short term as a humanitarian crisis, but in the long run, it's a very different problem. The refugee represents the loss of a significant investment in human talent. Countries invest in their citizens by providing some level of access to education, healthcare, and jobs. Often those who have the means to leave are the ones who have been invested in the most. They have the best jobs and educations, the most skills. They have the greatest social and political power. And when they leave, they take all of that with them.

Similarly, the church invests in its congregants, especially those who rise to positions of leadership. When the Dones walk out of the church, they take with them all of the institutional knowledge and training, all of their energy and talents, and all of their community and social connections that extend beyond the walls of the church. Our interviews indicate that the dechurched are among the most dedicated people in any congregation. They often work themselves into positions of leadership in an attempt to fix the things about the church that dissatisfy them before ultimately deciding their energies could be better spent elsewhere. In other words, the dechurched were the "doers" in their congregations.

ETHAN'S STORY

Perhaps the best way to get a sense of the general profile of a dechurched person is through Ethan's story. Ethan is a 47-year-old salesperson with three children. I met him on a spring day at a coffee shop near his office. He was initially reluctant, he said, to be interviewed because he still felt protective of the church and didn't want to be seen as trashing it. "Church leaders have been through a lot lately," he said. "Some of it's deserved, brought upon by their own actions, but a lot of it isn't. I think they're tired of getting beat up." He was eventually swayed by talking with his friend who had already done an interview with us and convinced him that we weren't really looking to point out the church's flaws.

His story is just one illustration of how embedded the dechurched often were in their congregations. He explained how, after a childhood of church involvement, he went to college and got involved in campus ministry before eventually making a career out of ministry and then abandoning the "flawed structure" of the church altogether:

> So I did campus ministry for years. I learned how to preach, I learned youth ministry, learned biblical counseling, and when I got out I went back to my old church, and they hired me as their youth pastor. Then I did assistant pastoring for three and a half years there, and I ran a youth drop-in center that was sponsored by United Way, where we tutored kids and had organized basketball, volleyball, field trips, and that type of thing. I did youth group for the church, and I led worship, and I led weddings, burials, and that sort of thing. For years I did all of that.
>
> When I left after a scandal with the head pastor cheating on his wife, we attended another church a few towns over, and I

was helping with the youth group there, and then they offered me a position. For the next six years, I was an associate pastor, and we did all the adult Christian education, children's ministry, led worship, pretty much a little of everything. From there it was on to Florida following my wife's job and on to another church which dissolved because the elders were stealing church money, and then out to Colorado, where we got involved again. We just can't help getting involved when we have talents to offer and we see a need, I guess.

Since 2010, though, when we finally left the church, we've just done house church where we create and do things *with* others rather than *for* them. I'm done with the top-down, institutional church. I thought we could fix it from within, but we got beat up pretty bad. I know we didn't always handle things the best way, but at the same time, we kept showing up and volunteering because we felt the church was God's home.

I don't think that's the case anymore. The church is wherever God's work is being done, and too often the way we were treated and the things I saw happen in the institutional church to other people just weren't in alliance with what we thought God wanted.

But here's the thing: I don't think the institutional church is filled with bad people. I think the church in America is an inherently flawed structure that compels people to make poor decisions. You're basically judged on how well you can preach and the numbers you bring in. *I realize the church isn't perfect, and it's made up of people who aren't perfect, and I'm not perfect either, but the church needs to see that there are things that are broken about the structure, not the people.* (Emphasis added.)

I offer this extended excerpt from Ethan's interview because it's representative of nearly all of the stories we heard. Although not everyone we talked to was involved in paid ministry, nearly all of them rose to a position of leadership during their years in the church. Often this happened in a way that's eerily similar to Ethan's experience. They would get heavily involved in a particular congregation, move for some reason or another and gradually, though not intentionally, begin taking on leadership roles at the new church. At some level, this speaks to the crushing organizational demands of running a congregation in today's religious landscape. Talent is hard to come by and resources even more scarce. It's only natural that a congregation would latch onto dedicated, experienced, and talented people.

However, Ethan's story and the dozens like his reveal something about the kind of people who generally make up the dechurched. They display an extreme level of dedication and devotion to God and religion, and they earnestly believe that the institutional church can be fixed and reclaimed. They believe it's worth fighting for right up to the point where they don't.

Ethan's involvement with organized religion eventually ended for the same general reasons that will show up again and again in the following pages. When I asked him what led to his eventually leaving the church, he simply said, "At first it was just survival, man. Spiritual survival. We had to get out." This language of spiritual abuse and survival represents a nearly constant theme running through our data. People put up with a lot of abuse before finally feeling the need to flee in order to keep their spiritual selves alive.

In many ways, it's this dynamic that's really at the heart of this book. How can the church possibly hope to survive and thrive as a relevant and meaningful social institution if it keeps spitting out Ethan and people like him? If people who are so dedicated to the church feel the need, ultimately, to leave for their own survival, what does that say about the church and its future?

Ethan became a religious person without a home when he and his family left institutional religion, forced to flee for his own spiritual survival. His response, creating and doing a house church, is both an indictment of institutional religion in America and a clue about where it might be headed. He and his wife didn't give up on God; they gave up on the institutional expression of church. They didn't stop doing things to advance what they believed to be the work of *God*; they stopped doing things to advance the work of the *church*. Their substantial energies and skills are now poured daily into activities and structures that happen completely outside the purview of organized religion. They've opted for relationship over structure, doing over dogma, and creating *with* rather than creating *for*. In short, they've created a new religious home.

> **They've opted for relationship over structure, doing over dogma, and creating *with* rather than creating *for*.**

This imagery returns us to the metaphor of the refugee. In a 2014 interview for World Refugee Day, Thuyet Nguyen, a 35-year-old Vietnamese refugee, was asked if it was important to stay connected to his country of origin or culture. He responded by drawing a distinction between the two, saying, "My culture, yes…My birth country, not so much…We are creating our own culture here, and it's something that is unique and beautiful."

As Mr. Nguyen demonstrates with his own experience and the research about refugees backs up in a more systematic way, people will abandon their countries when they're forced to, but they will retain their culture. Similarly, the dechurched have a strong desire to retain Christianity as a belief system and an equally strong desire to create a new culture of Christianity, but they're willing to abandon the church if it becomes necessary for their own survival.

Because of this, the dechurched movement represents a serious challenge to the church. Though we have every reason to believe the dechurched movement is large and growing, the numbers aren't as important as the type of people who are likely to become dechurched. In short, the dechurched are the people who do things, and without them, the church comes perilously close to losing relevance for people who want an active and engaged faith.

For years the church has laid almost exclusive claim to the energies and talents of faithful people. Years ago, if a person like Ethan wanted to be actively engaged in his community, the church served as one of the few outlets to organize such activity. It served as an important conduit for social activity. But this is not the case today, when people are increasingly connected in a myriad of ways that supersede the organizational capacity of the church. As Ethan demonstrates, people don't need the church to engage in meaningful community or religious activity. They can and are creating their own culture.

The Dones might lament the loss of the church and grieve the abandonment of an institution they once loved and were so hopeful for, but that won't stop them from actively expressing their faith. As one respondent, Ava, told us, "There's pain in leaving. There's loss. But there's hope, too. We're able to *do* things now."

There's real reason to believe, then, that in the future, religious activity in America will happen outside the bounds of the institutional church. As has been made extremely clear to us throughout the course of this research, there's a strong *desire* among our respondents for church, but there's no longer a *need* for church. The dechurched are tenacious and resourceful, drawing on their immense networks, knowledge, and training to engage in meaningful activity. They're finding ways to be the church outside of the institution.

In the future, religious activity in America will happen outside the bounds of the institutional church.

But the church will survive these challenges. Indeed, the church in America has survived much more significant challenges than those it is currently experiencing. The question is not whether the church in America will exist in 25 years. The question is entirely about what form it will take. Will it be a vibrant institution engaged in the meaningful issues in people's daily lives, a vital and indispensable guide in their struggle to make meaning out of life? Or will it be a curious outpost on the cultural landscape, serving only its own believers with an outmoded and out-of-touch social message?

The question is not whether the church in America will exist in 25 years. The question is entirely about what form it will take.

Ashleigh and I are simultaneously hopeful for the church and concerned about what the empirical data here and elsewhere tell us. Our personal preference is for a church that's engaging, important, and vibrant, but as scientists we can't ignore the data, which paint quite a different picture for the future of the Christian church in America.

Understanding how the church manages to drive away already committed believers, to make dechurched people out of churched people, is a necessary step toward charting a new future for the church in America.

ABOUT THE STUDY

This study draws on nearly 100 in-depth interviews with people who have made an active, deliberate decision to leave the institutional church.

We use the terms *dechurched* and *Dones* interchangeably throughout this text to describe these people. We had the privilege to catch people in all stages of the disaffiliation process. We talked to people just as they were about to leave, in some cases during their last weeks in church, and to others as they were tentatively trying out new congregations at the behest of friends or family members. The vast majority of our respondents, however, had been out of church for a while before talking with us and were not actively looking for a new faith community. Some of our respondents have since returned after a hiatus, but others have determined never to attend church regularly again. While everyone's story is unique, there are some common tensions that emerge among the dechurched.

- They wanted community…and got judgment.
- They wanted to affect the life of the church…and got bureaucracy.
- They wanted conversation…and got doctrine.
- They wanted meaningful engagement with the world…and got moral prescription.

Although our interview guide was crafted to allow for as much open conversation as possible while still staying on topic, these four contradictions came through time and again when we analyzed the data. People who had virtually nothing in common other than their decision to leave organized religion ended up telling remarkably similar stories centered around these four themes. As sociologists, this indicates to us pretty strongly that this phenomenon is not due to a few misfit personalities or bad church experiences. Rather, given the consistency in the data, we are reasonably sure that the dechurched phenomenon is directly attributable to a pattern that exists in the organizational and leadership structure of many, if not all, congregations in the United States.

However, we don't find any reason in the data to believe that these patterns are new. Just the opposite, in fact. Instead, what accounts for the rise in the dechurched is old ways of doing the "business" of church combined with new, contemporary understandings of what church is and should be. As our respondents show when discussing these tensions, the failure of the church to adapt to new cultural realities is a fundamental issue driving the dechurched movement. In short, what worked for churches to attract and keep people in the 1980s or 1990s can be the same practices that drive people away in the 2000s.

We take up each of these tensions in Chapters 2 through 5. What emerges is not only a more nearly complete picture of why seemingly engaged and committed people would leave the church, but also what can be done to repair that damage and prevent growing numbers of churchgoers from becoming dechurched. The importance of community, conversation, and meaningful activity come through clearly in these chapters.

In Chapter 6, then, we turn our attention to understanding how a congregation can be the church that nobody wants to leave in the first place. Drawing on the data presented in Chapters 2 through 5, we describe practices to avoid and those to encourage to keep people engaged, happy, and healthy in their home congregations as they grow and progress through their lives of faith. In that chapter, and indeed throughout the book, we report only what the data tell us. We avoid taking personal stances in favor of relaying the collective wisdom of our research participants.

As useful as these strategies are, however, they don't address the already substantial issue of the dechurched who currently exist. What, if anything, can be done to bring these people back to church? Is the work of God advanced more substantially by this group of dedicated outsiders, or is there benefit for everyone in trying to reengage the Dones? We address these questions as well in Chapter 6.

In the final chapter we bring all of this research together to argue that more than anything what the dechurched want is a home in the truest sense of the word. A place that's safe and supportive and refreshing and challenging. An identifiable place, embedded in a larger community where they both know and are known by those around them and where they feel they can have a meaningful impact on the world. They long for the same kind of church that we all long for. They desire a church that's active and engaged with the world, where people can bring their full and authentic selves and receive love and community in return. Without a church home, the dechurched wander the religious landscape often forgotten and unaccounted for by the both religious practitioners and scholars. This book is an attempt to collect their stories into a cohesive and understandable unit.

CHAPTER 2: COMMUNITY AND JUDGMENT

THE IMPORTANCE OF COMMUNITY

Perhaps more than anything else, what people want out of a church is a community of people who are experiencing God together. The dechurched are no different in this respect. Throughout our interviews, the dechurched told us time and again that they valued community above all else in a church. In fact, Liam explained that "it was the community that we developed there that kept us in for the longest time." He went on to tell us that when that community started to dissolve, it made it more and more difficult to put up with the rest of church. In other words, a sense of community is so important that it will keep people in churches that they don't otherwise care for.

This devotion to community also makes it much more difficult for the dechurched to casually shop around for churches. Mark, a 34-year-old former atheist, explained it this way:

> I only stayed in that church for so long because of the connections. It was the church that brought me from being an atheist to being a Christian. I had an affinity for the people there. I don't have that anywhere else. I wasn't going to walk away easily. I couldn't just go and look for another church, because it's not that easy for me. I would have to go and look for a whole new community. You can't just get that by looking at a church's website. The idea of trying out a new church is exhausting. It means, for me, trying out and investing in a whole new community. But it remains the biggest argument for me going back to church, to be with other people. The biggest drive for me is just to be able to experience Jesus

with other people in a community. That's really the only thing that could get me back.

The Dones place value on relationships and communities for a variety of spiritual and religious reasons. Community, for them, is synonymous with church when church operates the way they think it should. But much of the way they feel institutional church tries to construct community, by focusing on uniformity over unity, is counterproductive to what they feel is true and authentic community.

For example, when we asked Harper, a 43-year-old missionary who had recently graduated from seminary, about the importance of community, she told us, "It's very important. My husband is Australian, and it's a commonwealth where legally the good of the group trumps the good of the individual. When I look at the church, it should really be more like this. It's the heart of what is really good, which is to love your neighbor and care for you neighbor's well-being because you don't advance one without the other."

Harper's indirect reference to Jesus' great commandment was repeatedly brought up in our interviews when people talked about community. Our respondents often claimed that church should be a place where people are loved collectively rather than judged individually.

> **Our respondents often claimed that church should be a place where people are loved collectively rather than judged individually.**

THE CHURCH AS FAMILY

Mia told us that when church was best it was "more of an extended family and extended community, and that's what I like about church." She was choosing her metaphor here carefully, she told us. Families are not always harmonious or in agreement with one another, but in good, healthy families, there's always an understanding that the members are there for each other. That's what Mia likes about the church-as-family metaphor. And this makes sense, because church often serves the functions of an extended family.

In fact, when sociologists talk about social institutions as the building blocks of society, religion takes a vital position. The family is clearly the most important group in this respect, but religious groups often run a close second, providing stability, security, accountability, and a sense of morality in ways that other social institutions, such as education or the media, are just not capable of.

Indeed, religious groups are well poised to step in and fill many of the functions of a family in the event that the family or extended family can't or won't. Olivia, a 35-year-old college professor, gave just one example of many similar stories we heard. Even in the course of telling us how and why she ultimately left organized religion, she was able to recount a time when her church played a vital role in her life. She didn't grow up in the best home environment, and the church became a place where she got the love and care she wasn't finding at home.

She recounted her experience of feeling trapped by an abusive home life and the comfort and solace she found in her religious community:

> I would go to bed crying some nights, especially if my mom came home drunk or I knew she was drunk. And one night in particular, I was studying for the ACTs, and I had to get up really early to drive an hour because they didn't administer them in my hometown. My parents had people over that night, and they were partying and screaming and all of this stuff late into the night. I came out of my room, and I was like, "Can you please be quiet? I have to go take the ACTs tomorrow." And they made fun of me. It was horrifying. I will never forget that...But the church was, at that time, a safe haven from all that crap that I think I should not have had to deal with. They were really there for me during that period of time.

Pay close attention to what Olivia is saying here. She didn't look to the church to replace her family or turn to the pastor to be the authority figure she was missing in her life. She saw the church as a kind of family because the people there were loving. Church was a "safe haven."

Churches have often played this role. In fact, there isn't another social institution powerful enough to step in and take over the role of the family when the family is failing. Olivia is quite certain that if it weren't for her church community, she wouldn't have made it to where she is today.

In other words, religious organizations are extremely important social institutions. This is generally true across societies, but it's perhaps most true in the United States. Religious participation here is both voluntary and widespread, which means people have ample opportunities to form communities of trust where they can count on powerful bonds to sustain them through hard times.

FINDING GOD IN COMMUNITY

The dechurched who participated in our study placed great value on the church's traditions, liturgies, music, and other ways of connecting with God on a corporate level. However, it was in the smaller, more tightly knit, micro-level interactions that their faith and spiritual lives were really nurtured. When they left, they experienced sadness at the loss of the rituals, but they felt grief bordering on devastation at losing the connection with God that came through their church communities.

Elizabeth is a 67-year-old retired schoolteacher. She describes these sentiments while hinting at her sadness about the loss of the community she once treasured:

> I think what I crave more than anything else is not the music I loved or the building, which I also loved, and, you know, I love the service and the ritual. At our Methodist church, our pastor was German, and we had kneeling benches, and I like that ritual of kneeling for prayer. I like that ritual part of it. But as much as I loved those things, what I definitely crave and long for is the community that created and gave life to those things. But that was years ago. Today things are so divided and judgmental, especially around superficial issues, that I can't go into a church and pretend anymore to be someone I'm not. I have tattoos. I drink. I curse. I don't think any of these things make me a bad person, but lots of people at church do. I don't miss what it became, but I miss what I had.

It was clear that recounting these events to me, years later, still produced intense sadness. It's not that she used to miss her church community or that she was sad for a while and then got over it. She *still* misses it and is *still* sad. It was, clearly, an important group of people to her. However, she experienced the one thing that's the death blow for community: judgment from peers. When judgment creeps into a social group or community and isn't combated, the end is near. More on that later.

For now, we need to focus on understanding that leaving a church community is a loss, because religious communities are often composed of intense, personal, and intimate relationships. Thus, even when these relationships become dysfunctional, as in Elizabeth's case, people leave with remorse, sadness, and longing, but not bitterness.

As we draw on the metaphor of the refugee to frame this book, we can understand why people might long for a homeland even if they never or rarely knew a life of security or stability there. They long for home because it's home. It's their community, and it's filled with a lifetime of meaningful relationships. It's the place where they see familiar faces and are invested in the lives of the people around them.

My wife made this point clear to me one day as we were talking about the children of our friends in our own community. She said, "These are the kids that I'm so excited to watch grow up. I can't imagine ever leaving here." I can't think of a better way to describe the power of being embedded in a community. Birthday parties, graduations, struggles, and joys become a fundamental part of the way you choose to invest your emotional capital. These are the lens through which you imagine your future.

People who leave church feel the same way. The sights and smells and sounds are important, but it's the people and relationships that our participants kept telling us could never be replaced. They've invested too much of their time, efforts, and identity to walk away without sadness.

Mia and Olivia both remarked that church has the ability to be a community unlike any other. It can act as an extended family, providing love, comfort, and support. And it can breathe life into otherwise dead, disconnected, or meaningless rituals and activities. They felt that rituals, when done as a group, actually connected them to the divine.

And this was not true only for our respondents. Sociologists began studying religion in the 1800s, and some of their earliest and most enduring writings are about the power of community to transform ritual into meaningful activity. What seems to matter most is not the specifics of the ritual, but doing it together, with people who are known and trusted.

Emile Durkheim, one of the founders of sociology and one of the first people to pay attention to the role of religion in society, even went so far as to claim that engaging in collective ritual is a fundamental part of the creation of society.[1] Without shared experiences and common values, there is no ability to collectively organize. Religion, obviously, plays a central role in this process.

---

[1] Emile Durkheim, *The Elementary Forms of the Religious Life*, 1912.

The sense of community that our respondents found in church wasn't only among the highlights of their churchgoing experiences, it was also often at the core of why they began going to church in the first place. Theological conversion didn't spark church attendance; rather, relationships and community revealed God to them, and conversion followed.

> # Theological conversion didn't spark church attendance; rather, relationships and community revealed God to them, and conversion followed.

Mason's comments illustrate what many of our respondents told us:

> I've always been more about relationships. Like in high school in the midst of hating church, I connected with some of my best friends. We were all struggling to figure out what was going on with life, and so we would get lunch after they went to church, and we'd talk about stuff. It actually became pretty routine, and those meals led to a sense of belonging and fellowship. And so even in college I'd go places with people all the time simply because they'd invite me, and I was like, "Sure," and we'd talk about things and connect. I'd go with them and to some extent I didn't really care what we were doing, because I was with people I connected with. In college it finally dawned on me that these people all shared a common faith. Gradually we all got involved with Young Life, and I became a Christian. That was probably the first time I was part of a community, not Young Life, but those people. For me, they were kind of like my first home.

Did you catch that? Mason said this group of people, who were all Christians, were "like my first home." He didn't say that a church was his first home or community. He even clarified that he wasn't talking about Young Life, a parachurch youth ministry. Rather, he focused on the relationships. His loyalty and dedication, then, were to those relationships.

Mason's experience was not at all uncommon. Where Mason indicates that he always knew the people he was involved with shared the same faith, other stories revealed that even this basic level of agreement doesn't have to exist if there was a strong sense of community and relationship.

Michael explained a similar experience. The only prior experience he had had with religion had been his father-in-law's jailhouse conversion to a fundamentalist, Christian faith after years of agnosticism. Michael expected the same thing would happen to him. "That's what I was expecting: to see the light and go 'Oh, my God!'"

But that conversion moment never came, at least not in that way. It wasn't until years later, after a lot of congregational switching and church shopping, that he and his wife found a church community through some friends at work with whom he already had relationships. "They weren't trying to evangelize us; it just became that we were doing so many things they were doing that it made sense to do that thing, too."

Years later, Michael and his wife had to leave that church when work called them to a new city, but he took that sense of community with him. In fact, Michael and his wife would go on to eventually leave organized religion altogether when they concluded that the community they had in their old church was an anomaly. Although they tried, they weren't able to replicate that sense of belonging in a new church.[2]

"THE PEOPLE KEEP ME COMING BACK"

A strong sense of community kept many of our respondents in church even through hard times of transition in their congregations. It kept them working on behalf of the church, often for little or no pay, year after year. Being a part of a community was enough reward on its own.

When Ashleigh interviewed Jacob, a 40-year-old real estate agent, he was on the fence about leaving his church. He reached out to us because he was wondering how others had managed the transition. During the course of the conversation, she asked him what kept him hanging on. She expected to hear an answer about the value of what he was learning from the sermon each week or that his church provided an opportunity to do the kinds of social justice work he was interested in or something about the sanctity of the church experience. Instead, it was the relationships that drew him back.

---

[2]These stories might lead people to think they should focus on the relationship first and then to tell the message of Jesus afterward. As we discuss in Chapter 6, the Dones consider this approach dishonest and disingenuous. Instead, our respondents told us the focus should be on relationships first and always.

"I've thought about leaving," he said. "But then I think about the people I like there, and it's the only time I see them. So they keep me coming back." Jacob is devoted to these relationships. Nothing indicated that he idolized his community in the Christian sense of that word. He didn't put his desire for friends above God. Rather, he explained that he found God through them.

Jacob's story begins to hint at something that will become clear throughout this book. Namely, community is so important that it's often the only thing our respondents miss when they leave, and it's the first thing they seek to re-create outside of the church.

Think about that for just a second. The people who are leaving church are saying that the only thing they miss and have difficulty re-creating when they leave is a sense of community. In a time in which spiritual fulfillment is available in a variety of forms at any time of the day, what the church truly has to offer, according to the people who have left, is the ability to form and foster spiritual communities.

From an organizational perspective, that would indicate that time and resources spent on nurturing and sustaining communities would be well spent. But I don't think many, if any, of the churches I've observed in my years of doing research with congregations actually devoted a significant portion of their ministry resources to community formation. Furthermore, I don't think pastors and religious professionals have near the training in this area that they do for other parts of their jobs, such as budget management or sermon preparation.

Community is important to our respondents because it, more than any other single thing, is their connection to God. They not only find affirmation, support, and cheerleading in their communities; they also desire and seek diverse communities that foster accountability and include people who will challenge their fundamental beliefs. It's through these interactions that they experience the divine and gain a better understanding of their faith.

Thus, while community formation and relationships are important, it would be inaccurate to suspect that the emphasis our respondents place on community means that church was simply serving as a social club of sorts. While religious organizations do often form the basis for social capital formation, our respondents didn't lament the loss of their connections or feel the effects of the disintegration of their networks. Neither did they express a desire to form a new set of people they could call on in times of need or even to hang out with socially. Instead, they emphasized community from a distinctly religious perspective, explaining that they understand Christianity through interactions with others and a commitment to share life fully and honestly with a group of people. Community was fundamental to their understanding of God. They understood community as a manifestation and extension of their understanding of the divine.

Community was fundamental to their understanding of God.

Charlotte, a 53-year-old who lives in New England, shed light on this when she said:

> I don't think it's healthy to just stay inside the walls of a church. Being outside of that structure means having a much broader understanding of the world, a broader vision. I rub shoulders with so many different kinds of people now and have different kinds of relationships, and I really think that's how God intends us to be, to live in this world. We share things together and struggle with each other in a way that doesn't require agreement, just commitment. God doesn't want us walling inside, just being with each other, but that's what my long experience of church was like. And that would be the other reason I'm very hesitant to ever be a part of a church again, because I don't want to get stuck inside walls and miss out on all of these relationships that form the basis of my understanding of God.

Jaden provided an excellent illustration of this relationship between community and the sacred when he recounted how a genuine sense of community is what first drew him into the church and convinced him to come back after a period of being dechurched.

> I really enjoy the accountability aspect of my church. They hold people to a pretty high standard...I really enjoy the small groups and living in a community with one another. It's a big church of about 10,000 people, but they really, really, really pushed small groups and community and accountability, and so that was actually what we were looking for when we came back [to church]...Maybe I'm wrong, but that community aspect is really at the heart of my understanding of what God wants from us.

According to Jaden, he and his wife weren't in the market for a new church, having given up on organized religion some time ago for reasons that are pretty similar to those of our other respondents. They were done because of the politics and infighting and constantly being asked to do things to keep the church running. When their original small group dissolved as people moved away, they figured they were done for good. The church provided virtually no help through the transition, and that left a bad taste in Jaden's mouth. But they were drawn back in via a small group, because they already had friends who were involved with the small groups, and Jaden and his family longed for the relationships and accountability their friends were experiencing.

Jaden's comments echo those of many of our respondents: Community could be found in big churches and small churches, but it never happened accidentally. Community must be worked at, nurtured, and nourished. It's a misconception to think that community naturally occurs when people get together often enough or that community occurs when people who agree with each other come together. Community happens when people share life together, when they see each other repeatedly and share experiences. These commonalities lead to a feeling that people can be counted on and to a shared sense of reality and values.

Sociologists have long understood these to be the fundamental traits of community formation, but for some reason churches seem to often get this equation backwards. Instead of understanding that shared life leads to shared beliefs, churches frequently want to make sure that everyone signs on to a common belief system before they can begin to do life with each other. This is not only a dubious way to practice Christianity according to our respondents (see Chapter 4), but also a profoundly ineffective way to build community.

> Instead of understanding that shared life leads to shared beliefs, churches frequently want to make sure that everyone signs on to a common belief system before they can begin to do life with each other.

Think about the ways our respondents have talked about community throughout this chapter. They were drawn to churches that allowed communities to flourish and where relationships were available. They weren't drawn to churches because of a common or shared belief system.

In our interviews, we asked people how important it was that they agree theologically with the people in their church. Not one person said that it was very important, but nearly all of them told us that community was paramount. What we think this means is that these people are not expecting or desiring to join churches or do life with others just so they can have their beliefs confirmed or reinforced. What they want out of their communities is a commitment that people will be along with them for the journey.

If all of this assures us of the importance of community, it still leaves some questions unanswered. Perhaps the biggest of these questions are, Why is this sense of community so difficult to foster and create? What barriers stand in the way of creating community? And how can we do a better job in this area?

The answer to all of these questions begins with the issue of judgment. Elizabeth alluded to it earlier in the chapter, but the relationship between judgment and community, especially in churches, is complex. In the next section, we explore why judgment is so toxic to community formation and what can be done about it.

ENCOUNTERING JUDGMENT

The biggest obstacle to creating the kinds of communities our respondents long for is, quite simply, judgment. Our respondents uniformly expressed comfort with the idea of God as a judge (though they had very different ideas about what this would look like), but they were also unanimously opposed to people acting in this capacity. A feeling of judgment, in any social sphere, comes with dire consequences for a group. People who feel judged generally become defensive and withdraw from a group, but usually only after a period of gradual disengagement and resistance.

Take, for instance, Mason, who told us that judgment was a big part of his early church experiences:

> I've felt judged at all of the churches I've been to. I got in trouble at one church because I was wearing a hat. Sometimes the way I dressed or talked or when I painted my toenails in college. And also especially with regard to my gay and lesbian friends, my beliefs about homosexuality were not welcome. I have experienced that at Catholic and nondenominational churches as well as the mainline. I've learned now to keep my mouth shut around religious people. They're not *really* interested in what I think or have to say.

We learn a couple of extremely important things from Mason. First, we see that he has a true longing to be part of a religious community. Despite encountering judgment in all of those places, he kept coming back. He kept trying to find a group of people with whom he could be in community.

And we see something vitally important in his last sentence. Mason isn't looking for a group of people with whom he can agree. He never expressed, throughout the course of his interview, a desire to find people who shared his beliefs. Instead, he wanted a group of people with whom he could talk and exchange ideas. The alternative was to simply keep his mouth shut.

I suggest that when people begin thinking they can't talk to one another, the church has a bigger problem than could ever be solved by orthodoxy. Community without conversation, an equal exchange of ideas, is simply impossible.

> # Community without conversation, an equal exchange of ideas, is simply impossible.

There's also a feeling of being watched that comes with feeling judged. As nobody is perfect, this kind of surveillance only leads to uncovering more and more undesirable behavior among group members, and at some point, everyone is on the receiving end of the sword. The only way to avoid it is to constantly be the one wielding the sword, constantly on the attack.

Olivia, the 35-year-old college professor we met earlier, explained how she took every opportunity to point out the transgressions of others because doing so brought her in closer alignment with the group's professed beliefs.
She explained:

> I think one of the biggest reasons I feel I'm never going to go back to the church is because I was so judgmental. I judged my parents, all of my friends—everyone. I could never do that again because it feels terrible. I can't believe I did that to people.

This theme, of feeling judged for how well they did or didn't adhere to the beliefs set forth by their church, was a near constant among our respondents. In fact, judgment was so antithetical to the way they talked about community, that one could easily make the case that judgment is the opposite of community.

When we asked Alexander to describe his current beliefs to us, he made a distinction between community and judgment, which he feels is solely the territory of God:

> I believe that God desires us to be in community with one another and to learn from one another and to admit our sin and our depravity to one another. And to confess it to God as well and to seek his forgiveness.

Alexander is seeking a delicate balance. He thinks God calls us to be in community with one another and to admit our sins to one another, but he feels that God is the only one we need to seek forgiveness from. God is the only legitimate judge.

Judgment inherently lacks many of the religious elements our respondents hold as a core part of their belief system. Forgiveness, grace, humility, and love are absent in the moment of judgment, and those are the theological tenets held most closely by our respondents. While they expressed a wide array of beliefs about specific practices, such as baptism, or even on more fundamental doctrines such as the Resurrection, they uniformly understood Jesus as a source of forgiveness, grace, and humility. Not only does judgment fall short of these core Christian values that our respondents cherish and want to celebrate and see in action, but it's also highly ineffective in building community.

Forgiveness, grace, humility, and love are absent in the moment of judgment, and those are the theological tenets held most closely by our respondents.

Matthew made this point abundantly clear by describing a popular way some Christians he'd encountered had tried to profess love and judgment simultaneously:

Who would be interested if I said, "You're lost. You have no idea what you're doing in life, and you've really screwed up. But I love you and think you're great!"? My favorite is "Hate the sin; love the sinner." If you use the word *hate* in any way, shape, or form referring to something about me, I'm not going to listen. Who's going to listen to that?

Matthew pointed out that the important thing is not that people agreed with him, but that they understood him. For the Dones, these two positions, love and judgment, are simply incompatible coming from humans.

In fact, the negative consequences of judgment are so damaging that when our respondents talked about judgment, they never mentioned positive affirmation. They never told stories of people in the congregation judging them approvingly for their parenting or their patience or temperance. For them, judgment universally meant paying attention to, and calling out, undesirable behavior and attributing it to their inherent character. Nobody recounted a time they were judged to have acted poorly in a particular situation, but we heard lots of stories about people being judged as fundamentally flawed people who made poor decisions.

Our respondents frequently encountered these moments of judgment. In fact, as I sat down to write this section, I had planned to include some examples of the kinds of judgment our respondents described, but the list ended up being too long and, frankly, too depressing to include. However, it's worth pointing out that the judgment we heard about fell broadly into two types.

IMPLICIT JUDGMENT

By far the most pervasive type of judgment our respondents described was felt or perceived rather than overtly expressed. This typically occurred between congregants and included dirty looks, ostracism, jealousy, whispering, and rumors. These kinds of behaviors can be found in any social group, but they can be particularly damaging when they happen in church.

Furthermore, the fact that people are inclined to feel left out and criticized in a church setting—where they should expect to be warmly accepted, or at least given the benefit of the doubt—says something about the perceptions that exist about church and Christians. People are inclined to associate judgment with Christians. They're primed for it. As Liam told us before detailing a long list of times he'd felt judged as well as times he'd excluded and ostracized others, "Judgment in general is just a part of church."

Regardless of the accuracy of his claim, his perception is real, and church leaders would do well to be much more sensitive to these issues within their own congregations.

EXPLICIT JUDGMENT

Our respondents also encountered expressed judgment when people in the church encouraged them to change their behaviors or beliefs. These expressed judgments were often couched in biblical terms. This kind of judgment was often the domain of religious professionals who, no doubt, thought they were acting in the best interests of their congregants.

The trouble was not that our respondents viewed religious leaders as incapable interpreters of Scripture and God's will. The problem was that our respondents saw their religious leaders making lifestyle declarations and judgments without owning up to their own shortcomings. They viewed this as intellectually and morally dishonest, inauthentic, and an overreach of power. This kind of hypocrisy was probably the most damaging and produced the most long-term anger toward the church. To be clear, the dechurched who experienced this kind of judgment weren't thrilled about their leaders' transgressions, but the thing that drove them away (and kept them away) was their leaders' refusal to own up to their own failures and shortcomings while continuing to point out the flaws in others.

Jacob explained to us how he felt betrayed by his pastor after his mother's divorce. Although Jacob was in his 20s when the divorce occurred, he took it hard and felt betrayed by his pastor. His pastor had counseled his family both as a pastor and a family friend but stopped interacting with them when the divorce was finalized.

> I think, truthfully, the pastor is what turned me off of the church. He was one person in private and another person in church. And to me that's not acceptable...I was just like, "You're not the person you make yourself out to be, and I don't want to sit there and listen to you tell me how I should act when you don't act that way yourself." So I just quit going. In fact, I quit going for a long time after that.

When I asked Jacob to expand on this, he said:

> My pastor wouldn't marry a friend of mine in the church because he and his fiancée had lived together for six months before getting married. Yet my pastor had an affair with the woman across the street, and that was supposedly acceptable. Nothing happened to him at all.

Others gave similar accounts of pastors condemning the actions of congregants harshly, often publicly, while skating by when their own transgressions came to light: Women were asked to leave the church for being pregnant out of wedlock while the fathers remained, often in official church positions. People were asked to leave or repent for drinking alcohol and then ran into church elders at bars in town. Kids were told they couldn't bring their friends to youth group because they were a bad influence while other kids in the church smoked and drank on youth retreats. And on and on.

When we first heard these stories, we wondered if our respondents might be motivated by vindictiveness or a desire for their pastors to face the same judgment they'd experienced. But when we pressed them to explain why this disconnect between their pastors' words and actions bothered them, they expressed a quite different sentiment. What they really wanted was a shared understanding that we're all broken and in need of forgiveness and grace.

What they really wanted was a shared understanding that we're all broken and in need of forgiveness and grace.

Madison clearly summarized this sentiment:

> I hate the personal judgment that goes along with church. I know a lot of it comes from guilt, but since my relationship with God is really personal, I don't need a priest to tell me what I've done wrong. I already understand. I get it. We've *all* done wrong, including my priest.

Without that recognition, it sets up a false belief that religious leaders are beyond reproach, and such a belief is inconsistent with how our respondents understand their faith.

THE ROLE OF ACCOUNTABILITY

This distaste for judgment raises important sociological and religious questions. Have we become so narcissistic as a society that we only want to be around people who affirm everything we do? What are our religious leaders there for if not to hold us accountable to a belief system we've already professed faith in?

The answer to these questions returns us to the fundamental role of community expressed by our respondents. They didn't express a desire for unconditional support and affirmation. Instead, they wanted to be part of a group committed to working together in an environment of mutual trust to be the people God wants them to be while acknowledging that everyone will fall short of that goal.

As Madison made clear, the role of community is not to point out shortcomings. Our respondents were already acutely aware of their own failures. In fact, Layla, an 84-year-old lifelong churchgoer, recently stopped attending church because, she said, "I'm 84 and tired of being lectured to." But here's the thing: She still goes to her church's quilting group. She explained, "We just know each other. I can't imagine leaving them. We understand each other's lives. We don't always get along, but that's OK. It's like that with a family. But I'm just done with having some guy tell me what to do." These relationships, rather than an abstract version of authority that comes from the title "pastor," form the basis for accountability.

The role of a pastor, explained our respondents, should be to explain, rather than judge. Michael indicated that the focus on explanation at his new church is what brought him back:

> It didn't feel like I was being preached at. I was being explained to. Which to me is a big difference. When you're being preached at, it's a lot different from getting an education and learning. Learning is really what we should be doing at church. I don't think you should feel like you're being preached at and judged.

"It didn't feel like I was being preached at. I was being explained to. Which to me is a big difference."

This marks a distinct shift in pastoral style and skill set from what has defined the profession for much its history. Adjudication is simply not a desired part of the role; rather, communication, compassion, and context have become paramount.

COMMUNITY AFTER CHURCH

In order to understand the vital importance of community, it's necessary to look at what happens to people after they've stopped going to church. Our respondents made it clear that community was vitally important, and yet conspicuously absent in their churches. This passion for community translated beyond organized religion. Melissa told us, "I realized the people I knew who didn't go to church acted a lot more like Christians than the people I knew at church, so I started hanging out with them." When I pressed her to explain, she said she was looking for people who were loving, accepting, and forgiving, and that she was able to find those qualities in people who weren't churchgoers more easily than she found them in church.

Setting aside the sobering fact that Melissa's need for love, acceptance, and forgiveness wasn't met in the church, her comments reveal that she retained a desire for community. This desire didn't diminish or disappear when she left church, and her longing to be a part of a community that acted in ways that connected her to God didn't disappear either. She simply found another outlet to satisfy these needs.

Echoing Melissa, Mia indicated that perhaps the best way to be more Christian is to act less like Christians have tended to act:

Yes, we went to church, but we weren't involved. We were kind of dead ministers. Kind of going because we knew we should and hoping something would happen. But there was so much struggle, you know? When we separated, we stopped going to church, and I went to a Buddhist temple. The chanting made me realize, "No, God is God; Jesus is the Lord. I don't want to attend here." So I retained my Christian affiliation, but not my affiliation with Christians. If Christians acted more like Buddhists, they'd be nicer people. They're always judging. I really focused on wanting to be a nonjudgmental person.

"I retained my Christian affiliation, but not my affiliation with Christians."

Essentially, Mia not only encountered better people outside the church than inside, but she also felt *she* was a better person outside of the church. Olivia expressed similar sentiments earlier in this chapter, and Liam said essentially the same thing when he told us:

> Now I focus on a moral and loving God as opposed to a judgmental faith. It changes the way I deal with people, especially minorities and people of different faiths. I'm a much better person. This is a good thing for me since I work with diverse populations at my job on a college campus.

I also want to emphasize Mia's claim that she retained her Christian affiliation, but not her affiliation with Christians. This sentiment sums up the community life of most of our respondents after leaving the church. Very few of them disavowed Christianity. At the same time, very few of them held on to any explicitly Christian communities. When the Dones pursue community, they often do so with their Christian identify firmly intact, but not with the people who attend their old churches. They are done with church, but not with God.

Sometimes, these communities take the form of explicit worshipping groups, but more often they're simply groups who get together on a regular basis and do life together. Jason explained this as a movement:

> More and more I'm starting to see interesting and unique groups of people getting together, sometimes calling themselves churches, but they aren't attaching any meaning to the structure and the titles and the offices. The people are just getting

together and basically fellowshipping and looking into Scriptures, being there for each other. For my wife and me to come back, it would need to be like that—without religious expectations. If they were cool with us coming and hanging out and getting to know them and sharing our lives, that would be great. We would go to that.

In the meantime, they've found other ways to form community. Along with many of our respondents, they reported being much more involved in their community and civic organizations. They indicated that they had much more time for regular meals with friends. Some had even organized weekly meals, often on Sundays. When I explained to one of our respondents that his weekly meals sounded a lot like a church, he said, "You know, it sort of sounds like church when I explain it that way. A bunch of people coming together around a common meal to talk about life." But then he paused and said, "Nah. It's nothing like church. We all talk, and we all listen."

"It's nothing like church. We all talk, and we all listen."

It's important to remember that the dechurched are disproportionately people who were heavily involved in their churches. They're doers. And the desire to do things stays with them when they leave. They miss the ready-made communities that theoretically come with church, but they're quick to create their own communities around shared interests and common life experiences.

These comments suggest that a wholesale rethinking of the way we do church is necessary, rather than a few tweaks around the edges. In all of these comments, we see a desire, simply, for people to be nicer together. It became clear that after leaving churches, people go to great lengths to find community, but the one thing they won't put up with is the judgment they felt in church.

CONCLUSION

In order to keep people from leaving the church and to reengage those who have left, churches must do a much better job of affirming people while also going out of their way to explain, in word and action, that they aren't judging them.

This really can't be overstated. Judgment is associated with religion to such an extent that people simply assume they're being judged in church. I was talking about this issue with my graduate students one day, and one of them, who was still religious and had been raised in the church, said, "Oh, yeah, I've felt judged at church. Judgment is just a part of church."

Churches need to understand that they don't start from neutral in this respect. Right now, people assume their intrinsic worth and character will be judged, harshly and negatively, by religious people and organizations.

In order to reverse this perspective, corrective action must be taken. This doesn't mean affirming terrible behavior or advocating that people abandon morality. Rather, congregations and church leaders would do well to listen first, affirm second, and then listen some more.

> **Congregations and church leaders would do well to listen first, affirm second, and then listen some more.**

People want others in their community to hold them accountable, but they react violently when people outside their community try to do the same. Because religious leaders no longer have people's implicit trust, they aren't automatically part of the community. Before pastors or churches can act as a guide or moral compass for people, they must prove they're willing to be a fundamental part of their daily lives, struggling alongside them, building trust day after day.

We see ample evidence throughout this chapter that people are willing to engage in communities of accountability, but only with people who have earned that right by living with them, walking with them, and being in conversation with them on an ongoing basis.

We also see that people with long and active church histories don't need a pastor or church leadership to point out where they've failed or fallen short of God's will. They know. They've sat through countless sermons, Sunday school lessons, small group discussions, and Bible studies. They're acutely aware when they fall short of God's desire for their lives. When people in the church point out their failings, it simply feels like piling on.

What these people need from church is a community that will support them as they try to grow closer to God. They want support and help figuring out how they can live the lives they believe God wants for them.

CHAPTER 3: ACTIVITY AND BUREAUCRACY

Daniel spent years in the church as a worship leader and minister. He served in a variety of churches over the years, but it was his experience in his last church that ultimately shifted him into thinking there's something about the way church is organized that doesn't work for him. Here's an exchange from our interview:

Daniel: I see the institution, the hierarchy, the bureaucracy as crippling the body of Christ. I see it as creating this false dichotomy: If you really want to be influential and important and do something for Jesus, you have to go to seminary, you've got to get your degree, you've got to get ordained, and then you've got to get a microphone, and then you can start making a "difference" in the world. But that has nothing to do with what Jesus came here to start. Nothing.

Josh: That's a very strong position to take. Is there anything you miss about church?

Daniel: I miss the community that we had, that we could have had, I guess.

Josh: Have you managed to find anything post-church that fills that void or comes close to it?

Daniel: No, Josh, and the longer I'm gone, the more I grieve the loss of potential that was in that place. They were good people, but that structure just stifles people.

COMPELLED, CONFINED, AND COERCED

Daniel recognized that no organization can exist without structure, but he still found people's potential being stymied by the demands of the organization. Furthermore, he found it counter to his understanding of Jesus.

Daniel's frustration with organizations can be confirmed empirically. Sociologically, we know from over a century of studying these kinds of organizations that at some point, the bureaucracy takes over, and much activity in the organization ends up being geared toward its survival.

This works well in the for-profit world, but our respondents found this kind of structure incredibly off-putting in the church. They weren't frustrated by the existence of structure; they were frustrated when they felt the structure actively prevented them from doing the work they felt called to do. They were frustrated when they found themselves constantly and solely working to keep the organization going.

> They weren't frustrated by the existence of structure; they were frustrated when they felt the structure actively prevented them from doing the work they felt called to do.

All our respondents recognized that there is the business of the church to be done and that committees need to meet, but they shared a distinct sense that this often becomes the majority of what the church does—or, at the very least, the majority of what they were allowed to do in the church. The institutional barriers often got in the way of doing the work that people found to be truly impactful and connecting with God. As Ethan put it, "I was really into God, and the institution was in the way."

Years ago, a formerly dechurched person who had come back to organized religion at a small Protestant congregation said:

> We would rather spend time doing than spend time believing, if that makes any sense...At the last church I went to before this one, they just seemed to put up more and more walls and barriers. It got to the point that just to have a simple meal in

CHURCH REFUGEES

the church with some friends or a Bible study, we had to go through three committees. It just wasn't worth it anymore.

At the time, I thought this was an extreme example, but we encountered many of these stories throughout this project. The institution simply got in the way of doing the work of the church.

In this chapter we explore why the dechurched have given up on working within the institutional structures of organized religion. The central argument put forth here is that the dechurched are leaving because they wanted to affect the life of their congregation but encountered only bureaucracy.

This is a vital issue to understand, because the dechurched don't fit the typical burnout patterns that affect so many paid staff and overused volunteers in the world of ministry. Instead, the dechurched are walking away from church work, but not the work of the church. They're walking away because they're convinced that the structures and bureaucracy of the church are inhibiting their ability to serve God. They see the church as oriented only to its own survival. Instead of empowering, they find the church to be stifling. Over time, they've become convinced that their efforts and energies could be better spent serving God outside of the church.

> ## They're walking away because they're convinced that the structures and bureaucracy of the church are inhibiting their ability to serve God.

I think it's important to point out here that some institutional structure is necessary, and this book is in no way a call for the dismantling of organized religion. Our data don't suggest that such a dismantling would be desired or useful, and the research about organizational behavior wouldn't support such a call either.

Structure enables churches to coordinate schedules, track budgets, assign tasks, and a whole host of things that facilitate the work of the church and, among other things, often make newcomers feel comfortable and assured. Structure can assure a better use of time and money, promote more clarity and less confusion, and achieve greater reach and impact with limited resources. The benefits of organizational structure are numerous.

However, modern organizational theory compels us to recognize the dark side of structure as well. Heavily centralized and hierarchical organizations tend to concentrate power and gradually compel all activity inward, stifling innovation, creativity, and opposing ideas. This is not a problem unique to churches or religious organizations; these are problems inherent to all bureaucracies.

That's why it's necessary, from time to time, to critically evaluate organizational structures and processes to find out where they're working and where they might need to be altered.

I think that's the story here. The structures that dominate most churches work very well for the large segment of the congregation that's not particularly involved, or interested in being involved. But these same structures are not only ineffective for the most active members, they are actually driving them away. In this chapter and throughout this book, we argue that there's room to appeal to both groups of people, but it won't happen by accident. It will require a close examination and careful listening in order to understand what's working and what's not.

Daniel, the 50-year-old former churchgoer and staff member we met at the beginning of this chapter, described the bureaucracy he encountered at his former church:

> The continuous message at my old church was "None of us here have any name tags; there's no hierarchy; everyone is valued; leadership is shared; etc." That was the stated position, but it absolutely wasn't true in practice. In practice there were all kinds of gatekeepers and all kinds of hoops to jump through. And ultimately, you weren't going to get fully turned loose unless you were trusted and had passed some sort of invisible test. I know, because I was on staff there. I was a part of that process, but even I can't tell you how it happened exactly or why it evolved that way.

This is the tendency of all organizations and systems. Auto manufacturers hide faulty parts from consumers and top managers; space shuttles explode; countries are invaded based on faulty information. None of these things happens on purpose, as a direct result of organizational philosophy. Rather, groupthink, poor communication, concentrated power, and a host of other, identifiable flaws become embedded in every organization. The danger is in not recognizing those flaws and combating them constantly.

DESIRES OF THE DECHURCHED

As we state throughout this book, the bulk of the dechurched were extraordinarily active, committed members of their congregations. In fact, as we coded the interviews, looking for themes, the theme of church involvement came up more than any other topic or issue. It practically dominated our respondents' church histories. They simply couldn't tell their stories without talking about the things they'd been involved with as formal or informal leaders. They were the ones showing up early to set up worship spaces, attending planning meetings, implementing group decisions, leading Bible studies and youth groups, organizing retreats and outreach and small groups, and a whole host of behind-the-scenes things that make churches run and give life to community.

Aside from these informal leadership positions, a surprising number of our respondents held official titles within their congregations. They were elders, pastors, associate ministers, and the like. While this activity was occasionally paid—and we have a sizable group of former pastors (about two dozen) in our sample of the dechurched—most of this energy was poured into the church without compensation. It was sustained from a deep wellspring of desire and devotion. But even deep wells can run dry.

In order to understand the barriers to meaningful activity and what can be done to minimize or eliminate them, we need to start with an understanding of exactly what kind of participation the dechurched desire in the first place. They want to be active participants in their churches, but only if their participation can be meaningful. This is not to say that the dechurched are unwilling to engage in the mundane, daily tasks necessary to keep a congregation going. Instead, the tipping point comes when they feel those are the only tasks they're allowed to do.

Internally, they want to be involved in relationship formation and cultivation, and externally, they desire to be missional and impactful in their local communities.

Take, for example, Harper's comments about what she calls the "housework" of church. Harper is a 43-year-old urban missionary. She actually became dechurched throughout her time in seminary as she struggled to find an expression of organized religion that was outwardly focused instead of internally oriented. As she was undergoing her training, she became more committed to God but realized that she "didn't want to do the housework of keeping a faith group going. We were just interested in doing the relational work."

When pressed to explain what she meant by "housework," she said simply that it was anything focused on keeping the organization of the church running. To be clear, she wasn't saying that people should stop doing this work altogether; she was saying it just wasn't for her.

She wanted to expend her energy on something other than creating a weekly worship service, but she consistently found herself pressed into those roles in the various churches in which she had worshipped and served throughout her life. Eventually, she realized the issue was the structure itself, which was geared toward stability and growth over all else.

In response to this, she set out to find an alternative to institutional church. Later in this chapter, we'll describe the alternative she created, but for now it's important to consider why she wasn't empowered within the church to do the things she was interested in doing.

This theme came up often in our interviews. We heard powerful stories of people wanting to serve their local communities through efforts as simple as canned food drives to much more transformational neighborhood work that were ultimately stifled by the organizational dynamics and religious politics of their organizations.

KATIE'S STORY

Katie's story exemplifies this. I met Katie in the office of the nonprofit where she's the executive director. The building itself is simple and located in a rundown, mixed-use neighborhood that seems to have gotten stuck halfway through the process of gentrification.

As we sat around a simple folding table, she told me about her dream to start an art-therapy group in this inner-city neighborhood where she lives and where her former congregation is located. She had seen the need for an after-school program firsthand as her own kids went through the school system, so she decided to put her skills as a professional artist and licensed therapist to work in the neighborhood she cared about.

At first, she was hoping for some support from her congregation for supplies and materials, but eventually asked simply for space to meet. She showed me emails in which the church leaders expressed concern that her plan didn't include anything about getting the kids to become regular church members or to accept Jesus into their lives. Katie replied that a large number of the kids in the neighborhood were Muslim and that she didn't feel comfortable playing the role of evangelizer.

The church council took a vote and, on the pastor's recommendation, decided not to support the work she was doing because the kids weren't members of the church and might not even be Christians. Katie told me, "I just wasn't approaching it from that standpoint at all. I was on the other side of the transaction. I was on the giving side."

Eventually, Katie decided to start the organization as a nonprofit, and ultimately left her congregation.

> It just got to the point that it was so painfully obvious to me that the art therapy was making more of a real impact in the world, and was feeding me more spiritually as a group of people committed to relationships than my home congregation had ever done.

Her organization now employs half a dozen people, serves dozens of youth every week, and has won numerous awards for civic engagement. When I asked her to describe her experience of disengagement from her church, she said she would have preferred to stay, but she wasn't going to let the church get in the way of her calling.

Katie's story highlights a key theme that ran throughout our interviews. Namely, our respondents believe that the church as a building or an institution isn't necessarily the sole expression of God's will. As Katie recounted her feelings about the church, she was upset about the way things happened, but she never directed that anger toward God. She viewed her decision to follow God out of the organized church as an act of faith and lamented only the lost relationships within her congregation. Even so, she managed to replace those relationships with what she calls her family at her nonprofit.

Katie's story reveals the tension between a church worried about pouring resources into something that doesn't have an identifiable return on investment and a congregant who simply wants to act, to be "on the giving side," as Katie put it. There was nothing in Katie's plan that was geared to lead directly to more bodies in the pews or dollars in the collection plate.

THE CHURCH AS CORPORATION

Ethan and Jason separately confirmed that this tension was at work in their decisions to leave as well. They each told us about wanting to be engaged in meaningful activity, only to be blocked by layers of bureaucracy and organizational structure. They both left after growing tired of not being allowed to be true participants inside their own churches. While they were allowed to be involved, it was never on their terms. They weren't able to give life to the church or to shape its direction. Instead, they felt they were basically working as entry-level employees for a large organization.

In fact, this language of the church as a corporation with the pastor as CEO was used frequently in our interviews. Ethan told us he had freedom to do some things, but at the end of the day, decisions were made by one person, the senior pastor:

> It was like the senior pastor had 51 percent of the stock in the company. And nothing we wanted was really going to overrule what he wanted. So our only real choice was to either agree with him or disagree, but the same things were going to happen either way.

Jason echoed these sentiments:

> I know we had all these different ministries and activities, but in the end the pastor was the guy who made all of the decisions.

I asked both Ethan and Jason why they didn't simply switch to another church. As it turns out, both of them had tried many different congregations over the years. Seeing the same patterns at different stops was what finally did them both in. Jason ultimately decided to leave when he "realized it wasn't just me. It's kind of churchwide." In other words, he attributed this top-down, controlling leadership style not just to one person, but to the organizational structure.

In the end, Jason and Ethan came to the same conclusion that Katie reached. They all decided the structure, not the people, is the problem. If they were to engage in meaningful action in a religious system, it had to be in the context of a different system, not necessarily with different people.

Cole is a 46-year-old investor and former superintendent of a school associated with his church. He reached a similar conclusion:

> I just didn't want to be part of a system with a CEO pastor at the top and the rest of us just doing what he says. And it's not that my pastor is a bad person. He's a great man in a bad system. I'm not one of these guys out to destroy the institution, because in different seasons of life, I can see why people connect with it and get a lot out of it. I did for a long time. But it's just not for me anymore. There's nothing for me there. There's nothing for me to do there that's meaningful.

"There's nothing for me to do there that's meaningful."

This focus on the organizational structure helps to explain why, after years of engagement with organized religion in a variety of congregations, the Dones don't go looking for one more church. They're done with church in the relatively narrow, institutionalized expression that dominates our contemporary understanding of church. They've been dechurched. After determining that the structure worked primarily to sustain itself, they just couldn't see themselves walking into another one of those structures.

The problem, as they saw it, was that there was no true participation in their churches. People were either doing the things that the person or people in charge wanted done, or they weren't allowed to do much of anything. There was no freedom to truly shape their own community.

Ben returned to the language of the corporation to explain why this system was unfulfilling to him:

> It even affected me spiritually that the church was really large and very business-minded. It was very corporate just in how it managed people and how it set up programs. To me it was just like a big transaction, and the big thing, especially to me, is that it was very impersonal.

Ben was careful to qualify his comments as pertaining just to him, but we heard a lot of people express similar roots of dissatisfaction. In fact, we heard story after story from people who experienced this same disconnect between the way church was done and how they wanted to experience God, create community, and use their gifts. This theme was so common that we could reach no other conclusion than that the top-down hierarchy of worship- and ministry-planning not only alienated these committed volunteers and staff from doing church work, but it also alienated them spiritually.

In 2010, I wrote about this phenomenon in my book about the emerging church movement. Although that book is about a wholly separate set of organizational issues, I encountered many of the dechurched who had migrated to emerging church congregations. Many of those people expressed some misgivings about theological issues, but they were willing to push them aside because of the organizational appeal of a flatter hierarchy and more empowered lay participation.

All of these data have convinced me that there is a truly sizable subset of congregants, and the recently dechurched, who desire to be active participants in a community of believers but aren't willing to be the mouthpiece of someone else's vision. They want to be able to make meaningful decisions and participate as equals in their communities. Too often, they say, church staff and pastors are willing to empower lay leaders, paid staff, and volunteers to do meaningless, mundane, and unfulfilling work while the senior pastor retains all of the authority and ability to make creative, meaningful decisions on behalf of the congregation.

JASON'S STORY

Jason stated this position most powerfully, so I want to tell his story at length. It's emblematic of what we heard from so many others. Jason is a former pastor who has held a variety of roles in churches, including congregant, teaching pastor, music director, and youth director. While he hasn't always been involved in leadership positions, he and his family have frequently served in leadership capacities. He and his wife no longer go to church, though. It wasn't burnout or church politics that drove them away (though certainly those didn't help). Instead, it was a feeling that church structure and organization were getting in the way of communing with people.

> My whole paradigm has changed about why we get together, why we have groups of people we gather with, fellowship with—however you want to say it. I no longer buy into this idea of a hierarchical structure of leadership and people being in submission to leaders. That's a huge thing for me. When I get together with people now, everyone is on a level playing field; nobody is over anyone.
>
> Pursuing that ideal changed everything for us. Things are so different now. There was a time in my life when I thought church leadership was what I was supposed to do. I am supposed to be involved in some kind of full-time Christian ministry. My actual giftings are art and music, so it was a big thing to take over the music in our church, and I ended up being an elder. When I got in the position I was supposed to be in after years

of service and sacrifice to the church, I felt completely empty and that it was all meaningless. That was when I started to ask a lot of hard questions and started to step away, but it was a process.

Jason didn't bristle at the notion of authority; he was bothered by the *execution* of authority in the church even as he himself wielded that power. He felt the structure kept him from engaging others in meaningful ways and finding God in the process. He left the church when he realized he was pursuing a position in an organization rather than people in relationships. Jason's story once again reveals what so many respondents echoed: They left because of structural problems, not issues with people.

> ## He left the church when he realized he was pursuing a position in an organization rather than people in relationships.

If there is a real desire to retain active and committed congregants and appeal to the dechurched or soon-to-be dechurched, pastors and paid staff should spend much more time doing the mundane daily chores of keeping a congregation running, while including others in setting the creative and spiritual agenda.

UNNECESSARY BARRIERS

Throughout my career as a sociologist, I've seen that people are acutely aware of organizational forces and dynamics. They display a sophisticated understanding of organizations and the ability to separate the organization from the individual.

While we certainly heard many stories about individual people acting poorly, we also encountered numerous examples of dysfunction inherent to organizations. William, a 59-year-old counselor, deftly articulated the self-perpetuating nature of organizations and how they ultimately work to exclude rather than include people, voices, and ideas:

Systems will always preserve the system at the expense of the individual because the system is bigger and more important. If individuals don't fit the mission anymore, then they're destructive to that mission, and the organization will find a way to get rid of them. So I don't think organized church works, at least not in the ways that I've seen it. I think it works to have meals together, go to movies together, talk about what's going on in your life. If it's formal, and if there's a talking head, just shoot me because I really think that just breaks down. As soon as you organize it, you have to decide "Do we sing, or don't we sing?" "How do we pray?" "Do we light candles, or don't we light candles?" "Do we have art, or don't we have art?" "Will there be music?" "Who gets to play the instruments?" "Who can't play those instruments?"

Virtually everything William identified can be verified by academic research about the nature of organizations and systems. Certainly there are some organizational forms and practices that resist these tendencies better than others, but the way most churches are organized, as relatively centralized hierarchies, matches what William articulates. These same principles dominate organizations of any kind, whether in the field of religion, politics, or for-profit companies. With regard to religion specifically, though, these organizational practices can be especially damaging. Churches are generally thought to be a place where people come together in community. Bureaucracy and hierarchy inherently undermine that purpose.

Isabella, a psychotherapist who came to her profession after a long career as a pastor's wife, made this connection explicit when she said, "The thing that broke my heart was not theology. It was how people behaved in groups and how leadership behaved and how systems got corrupted."

> "The thing that broke my heart was not theology. It was how people behaved in groups and how leadership behaved and how systems got corrupted."

At every stop along her husband's career, she said, she encountered well-meaning people on staff who were engaged in activities that made it harder for regular congregants to have much control or power over anything. Isabella was not frustrated with any particular pastor or bishop; she was dismayed by the systems that compelled particular behavior from leaders and groups of people.

Many of our respondents picked up on Isabella's idea that bureaucracies compel behavior that's not always consistent with their understanding of Christianity. Allison, who spent her career as a systems expert in the aerospace and aviation industries, explained it this way:

> I spent my whole career designing systems in the for-profit world, and when I heard people in my church using the same language and concepts as my bosses and colleagues, that just sent up a huge red flag. They kept talking about efficiency and subcommittees and things. The problem is that when you pursue expediency in the church and try to be more efficient, the cost is always human, because the church relies on volunteers. You have to squeeze more time, energy, and money out of people or ask them to move aside because they don't reach the organizational goals that you've foisted upon them. It just leads to pastors acting like CEOs and treating churches like corporations and congregants as employees. That's a bad place for a church to be.

She went on to explain that she thought this was a bad model for church because it places unnecessary barriers between people and doing the work of God. Sometimes, of course, this happens in very heavy-handed ways, and we heard numerous instances of pastors simply saying "no" when somebody wanted to start something that didn't fit the vision laid out by the pastor. By far, though, the biggest and most insidious barriers were organizational and bureaucratic, the kind Allison alluded to.

CORA'S STORY

We heard far too many of these examples to recount each one in detail, but it's useful to examine one in-depth. Cora is 66 years old. She spent the majority of her 40s and 50s in the church before leaving about five years ago. She is, as she puts it, "one of those people who just goes 100 miles an hour in everything I do. I just can't sit still."

When I asked her to list the kinds of things she did in her former church, the list occupied nearly a page of the interview transcript. While she enjoyed most of these activities, she was continually frustrated, she said, when she tried to work on her own things or advance projects she was passionate about.

> It was fine as long as I was doing what I was told. As long as I was plugged into what someone else had put forth, it was no problem. But when I wanted to do something on my own, it was a different story. The last thing I tried to do was start a little group to help the elderly people in our congregation, where we would just go and mow lawns and wash windows and things for people who needed it. But that never came about. There were so many rules and regulations just to mow lawns that I backed off of it. It's weird, because we were such a big church you would think this little thing would be easy. But I talked to the missions minister, and he told me to come up with a name for my group, propose a budget, write a mission statement, come to the board hearing, and figure out a way to report back every month. I told him, "Really? I just want to mow lawns. Why do we have to do all that?" He told me the board didn't like things going on in the church unless they could oversee them. And here's the kicker: They weren't offering me anything in return. No budget, no help recruiting or organizing. It was just about control. So by that time, I was like, "OK, never mind. I'll just do this on my own."

The first question that came to mind after she told me this story was "How did the missions minister respond after you let the project drop?" I assumed he must have followed up with her since she was offering to organize a ministry in his church.

Allison just laughed when I asked about this. "Oh, no. Not at all. They didn't need me. I never heard from any of them again. Not once."

After all of this, though, Allison didn't conclude that he was a bad person or that the board was ill-meaning. She said:

> I get it. It's a big church. You need rules and regulations. But you should be able to be empowering, too. It's not their fault. They're just doing what they're supposed to do. But is that really what we're called to do?

Compare Allison's statement with Cole's comments about his former pastors and church council members:

> It's not their fault. They're not bad people. They're just part of the system, and this is what it demands to keep going. It's what they're trained to do. They're just trying to keep things going in the only way they know how.

Clearly, our respondents viewed the institutional expressions of Christianity as part of a man-made system that exists apart from any individual. They viewed it as a depersonalized machine or system that serves only its own purposes.

Sofia, a journalist and professor with her doctorate and a long history of church work in multiple congregations, told us a remarkably similar story:

> All of a sudden I didn't feel I had any reason to be there. I felt that really all I was doing was functioning as part of a machine, doing what the machine likes, which is money and head count. You know, do as you're told, think what we think, do what we want and need, and we're done with you. Nobody was mean to me; nobody did anything. It was like once you became a member, it was all about what you could do for the church to keep the church going.

In both of these accounts we get a sense that the structures don't restrict the range of possible decisions people *might* make in their capacity as staff members, but rather the range of decisions they're *likely* to make.

It's this kind of fundamental sociological insight that's missing from many pastors' understanding of church. While they often get massive amounts of training in theology, they miss some of the key sociological dynamics at work in their churches.

Our respondents understood the structure, not the people, as the source of their dissatisfaction, and that led many of them to opt out of organized religion in favor of something else. In the vast majority of cases, they opted out to do work that most people would say is church work.

However, this desire to leave the organization but still be a part of something comes with its own difficulties. Emily expressed the tension inherent in this position. She claimed, "At this point, I don't mind being a part of religion, but I don't want to be a part of *organized* religion. I don't want that formal structure."

Emily's position, in particular, raises the question, What does it mean to be a part of religion, but not a part of "organized" religion? What are these people, so turned off by the bureaucratic boundaries of the church, turning to when they leave organized religion? How are they creating religion outside of the organization?

> # What does it mean to be a part of religion, but not a part of "organized" religion?

ALTERNATIVES TO CHURCH

Perhaps the most important thing to understand about the post-church activities of the dechurched is that they're still very much engaged in the work of seeking the divine and living out what they believe to be God's will for their lives. In many cases, in fact, they're even more involved in these activities after being freed from traditional organizational barriers.

Their efforts are diverse and multifaceted, but they generally fall into one of a few categories, none of which is mutually exclusive. The dechurched tend to construct church alternatives through political and civic engagement, small groups or house churches, or informal but spiritually meaningful gatherings.

Of the scores of people we interviewed, only a handful replaced church with something they would consider nonspiritual in nature, like watching football on Sundays. The vast majority of our respondents still felt a strong pull toward God but needed a different avenue for spiritual expression and fulfillment.

This, in and of itself, is not necessarily bad news for the institutional church. Certainly a significant amount of religious activity has always taken place outside of institutional boundaries. However, we began to sense a shift in the religious landscape when we began to repeatedly hear of the kinds of things people were doing outside of church because they felt stymied in their attempts to do them inside of church.

As our society approaches a post-institutional era, it's entirely possible the near monopoly that the church has enjoyed over faithful expressions and religious connections may be coming to an end. The activities of the dechurched may be ushering in a new understanding of what religious activity means. If this trend continues, it will fundamentally reshape the way Americans experience organized religion.

Furthermore, the fact that our respondents felt they had to leave the church in order to do the things we outline in the following pages raises some fundamental questions about the role and relevance of the church in contemporary society. As you read the following profiles, we encourage you to ask yourself, "If this isn't the work of the church, then what is?"

POLITICAL AND CIVIC ENGAGEMENT

Earlier in this chapter, I described Harper's desire not to do the "housework" of keeping church going. Let's return to her story now to find out what she ended up doing in response to those feelings.

When asked what she'd been doing since leaving her congregation, she described a life of sacrifice and devotion to her local community and a strong connection to her faith. The following excerpt summarizes her motivations and explains why she felt that a traditional church was not the place for her and her husband to do the kind of work they felt called to do.

For years, they'd been part of a regular gathering of people that occurred outside of a traditional Sunday morning worship service. She explained why she and her husband were drawn to this structure and how they tried to keep it from falling prey to the same kinds of institutional forces they were trying to resist:

> My husband and I thought we should renew ourselves and get rid of this very strong church reflex to meet together on Sunday in any form. As long as that's in place, it will get our best, and that's no good. If you want to go to church on Sunday, then do that. There are lots of them that already exist. Go to another church. Use the resources that exist. Then let's meet monthly in people's houses and eat together and pray together and just be friends rather than just putting on a program for each other every week.

We live in a time of highly privatized, individualistic structures, so what we really wanted was to share and care for one another and contribute to the community's well-being, which involves knowing our local officials and being a part of our neighborhood association and participating in those civic structures. It was more important for us to participate in those civic structures than spend that energy on the church. It was the experience of faith applied seven days a week. It had an integrity that just going to church once a week and not doing anything about it the other six days didn't have for us.

When our community has a gathering, it's always a little crazy. Like, we always had mentally ill people with us and homeless people, and we never knew who would show up. It was really messy, and I think most people would have felt that it was odd. Anyone was welcome to come, no matter what we were doing. *It was badly organized on purpose*, because we didn't put our resources into the gathering.

We didn't put our resources there because we were just not focused on that. We were focused on the needs of the city. To us, every bit of energy spent on the worship service was energy that took away from that mission. Obviously, you can go overboard with that, and it's not for everyone, but it was certainly what we needed. And it was obviously what a lot of others needed, too.

Before continuing with Harper's story, I want to draw your attention to the emphasized phrase: Their gatherings were "badly organized on purpose." One of the consistent messages of this chapter and the entire book is that churches are very, very good at organizing and producing a lot of things that fundamentally don't matter to the dechurched. Churches are good at finding charismatic people to espouse compelling sermons, and they are equally adept at producing well-organized and well-executed worship services. Doing this, however, requires a tremendous amount of time, energy, and resources.

Harper and her husband made the choice to have poorly run services in order to do a better job of serving the poor. Larger congregations and groups may not have to choose one or the other, but the organizational scholar in me simply looks at resources spent.

In fact, take a minute right now to calculate all of the staff and volunteer time and monthly budget that go into producing the Sunday morning service(s) at your church.

I recently talked to a pastor of a church of about 100 worshippers. We added up all of the time it took to produce the service, prepare his sermon, produce the podcast of the service, set up, practice, and so on. When we finished, we figured his church was spending around 137 hours a week and a full 60 percent of its budget to produce the 90-minute service from 10:00 to11:30 each Sunday morning.

He was stunned. But neither of us thought that was particularly out of line with other churches we had seen or been a part of. Think about that for a minute. Thousands of dollars and hundreds of hours per month to produce four worship gatherings.

The problem is not the vast amount of resources that go into the service. Maybe you've decided that the gathering is what your congregation is really about, and that's fine. The problem is not being aware of reality. The problem is in claiming a missional and outreach focus, or a teaching and small group focus, when the vast majority of resources are spent elsewhere. From an organizational standpoint, this lack of understanding means, functionally, that it's very difficult to make room for worship, small groups, *and* outreach.

For their part, the dechurched saw this devotion to the Sunday morning gathering as a resource hog. They argued that it leaves precious little time, talent, and energy for other activities like the kind Harper and her husband were interested in. Like the kind that most of the people in our study were interested in.

The dechurched saw this devotion to the Sunday morning gathering as a resource hog.

Additionally, it leads to the very real perception that Sunday mornings are far and away the most important thing the church does, and it's hard to argue otherwise even if a large portion of both congregants and church leaders would tell you that it maybe should not be the case. Thus, Harper and her community made the decision not to organize their gatherings. They had enough collective church experience to know that perfecting a worship service is endless and all-consuming, because it can always be improved. Instead, they wanted to put the other parts of their faith first and take care of the gathering secondarily.

Harper illustrated this:

The church over the last 100 years has gone as institutions go. They become more cemented, and they gravitate toward maintenance, where they focus all of their energies on just keeping things going. Instead of existing for the world, they exist for themselves. And that, to me, didn't match the biblical narrative. It didn't match what I could see was needed and possible out in the world.

So we moved into a very low-income neighborhood, and we bought a house. We were much more interested in spending our time and energy and imagination serving and caring for and loving our neighbors. We started and maintained a community garden; we do after-school tutoring for kids. We work as neighborhood liaisons for our elected city officials, we do neighborhood walks to strengthen relationships, we work a lot with refugees, and a ton of other things. And that stuff was just never going to be a priority with my old church—not in any truly relational way, and I wasn't interested in just throwing money at the problem.

So it wasn't bad when we left, but honestly, I just didn't want to go to church. I wasn't interested in sitting in a room, hearing a message every week, and not having the ability to use the collective efforts of those people to do anything. I just wasn't interested in that. At this point, I would rather die than go to church, because it would mean giving up all that we've done here.

Harper connected her post-church activity directly to the institutional limitations of her experiences with organized religion. Furthermore, she sees the work she's doing now as fundamentally incompatible with her old, institutional church. She doesn't think the two could coexist, and she makes a distinction between doing the work of the church and participating in her neighborhood civic structures, volunteering, and working for the common good. *And* she's not making a big point of this. She mentions it casually, almost as a matter of fact. Somehow the church in America has given some of its most active and dedicated members the impression that church work does not consist of community gardening, bridge building, and working with refugees.

Perhaps the thing that comes through most clearly from her story and the dozens like hers is that the church needs to do a better job of making space for these people within their communities. This means reassessing where church resources are spent and limiting the amount of organizational space the worship service can occupy.

While Harper makes a general reference to the biblical narrative not matching a highly produced Sunday worship experience, it was Mark, a former pastor, who put it more succinctly. When asked why he left his role as a highly paid worship pastor at a large, suburban megachurch, his answer was simple: "I just couldn't see how any of this was necessary."

It was nice, he said, but it wasn't necessary. There were other things, such as hunger, poverty, and education that he considered necessary focuses for the church, but the church wasn't meaningfully engaged in them. While his church was doing some things in those areas, they consumed a tiny portion of the overall budget. And, even in his role as a pastor, he felt powerless to address this.

After our formal interview had concluded, he followed me out to my car and said:

> The machine just eats you up. Maybe other people could figure it out. Maybe I should have been better at my job, but I couldn't get the ship turned in that direction. There was too much at stake for the organization to change.

SMALL GROUPS AND HOUSE CHURCHES

Another way the dechurched found to express their faith after leaving mainstream, organized religion is something akin to house church. The important thing to understand about these gatherings, though, is that the form is less important than the function. The driving impulse is to bring people into relationship with one another.

Matthew explained:

> The big thing to me is to have people get together and talk in small groups. I've looked a little bit at house churches around here. That model intrigues me because it's relationship first, theology second.

We didn't find any evidence among our respondents that they were leaving churches where they had great relationships with people just because they hated the large, corporate worship gathering. Rather, they turned to house churches and similar gatherings because they found them to be the only way to cultivate the kinds of spiritual relationships they were after.

Ethan explained how he and his family came to a house church. He wasn't searching for a group of people with whom he always agreed. He was searching for a place where he could be a full participant and engage meaningfully in the activities of his worship and faith community.

> From 2001 on, all we've done is house church. We tried planting a few churches, but all I found was this top-down model that's just repulsive to us. This model of who has the best advertising, and it's all about Sunday morning. My experience is that churches aren't really that different. You either dress up or you dress down, but you go, and there's an order of service. Generally there's an opening prayer, announcements, the offering, then 30 to 40 minutes of preaching, a prayer, and you go home. We wanted relationships that just couldn't be formed, in our experience, in that structure.

Ethan worked for years within traditional church structures, even going so far as to plant his own churches for a while. But none of these models was able to provide what he was looking for. None of them filled him and his family spiritually and connected them to others in the way they desired.

Daniel, whom we met at the beginning of this chapter, also turns to changing structures as he tries to find what's next for him:

> I'm looking. I'm looking for something else. We've actually had some small home gatherings here, and we've done a couple of the home-type gatherings at other places. It just can't be the same as it was. It can't be that structure of church that everyone thinks about when you say "church." So I'm still looking, I'm still hoping, and I'm still yearning for something different.

Maria's experience was similar. She left the church but took her small group with her. The group that had originally formed around a very specific cause, a prison ministry, eventually morphed into a small group. When her church placed increasingly more restrictions on what they could do, the group ended up leaving the church. As Maria tells it, it was not a collective decision. Rather, over a period of months the members of the group found themselves being drawn more to the small group, which provided better relationships and less frustration than the church they were tied to.

REGULAR, INFORMAL GATHERINGS

The final common outlet for faith formation and expression among the dechurched we interviewed involved meeting regularly, but informally, with a group of people.

Most often this took the form of a weekly dinner or meal, but there were many other manifestations, including book clubs, movie-watching groups, online chat rooms, forums, and musical gatherings. While none of these experiences might seem inherently spiritual, our participants characterized them as expressions of their faith. That is, the people we interviewed explicitly understood these activities as different and set aside from the other things in their lives that might seem similar. To put it in sociological terms, they saw these things as sacred and opposed to the mundane, nonspiritual, daily activities that consumed the rest of their lives.

Remember Layla, the 84-year-old woman who gave up on church after a lifetime of attendance but is still involved in her church's quilting group? Quilting might not be holy work, but participating in this group is clearly holy for her.

When we asked our respondents what appealed to them about these groups as opposed to churches' organized small groups, they pointed again to bureaucracy. There were no hoops to jump through, no elder boards that had to approve or sanction their gatherings, and nobody to tell them when or how to get together. From a simple transactional perspective, our respondents had a difficult time understanding why they should be a part of the church when all it did was mandate regulation and provide very few or no resources in return. As Kelly said, "We were going to get together anyway, and the church certainly wouldn't have made it any easier for us." Basically, it was just easier to get together with people outside of church than inside of church.

> ## It was just easier to get together with people outside of church than inside of church.

Our respondents were turned off not only by the practical frustrations of the systems imposed by the institutional church, but also by their theological implications. They felt that the church should be facilitating gathering, not standing in its way. They weren't at all concerned about being exposed to ideas or theology that challenged them or that might not be in alignment with their own faith traditions.

Jeff explained that this was a theological issue for him. He stated his position this way: "The cross overcomes all. We're meant to be together. If we get it wrong once in a while, God will forgive."

This same perspective was embedded in many of the responses we got when we asked about an ideal church. The most common sentiment was that an ideal church would be a place where all people are welcome, and this was part of the fundamental appeal of these informal gatherings and groups.

Again in these stories we see a return to the concept of the reluctant leaver, which echoes back to the refugee. People are trying, sometimes for years, to make church work for them before eventually, reluctantly, moving on. And when they move on, they move to things that look nothing like the activities that consume the traditional church. They move on to community gardens, art therapy, meals in living rooms around a communal table, Internet chat rooms, and quilting groups. Nobody, not one single respondent, mentioned replacing church with a worship service or with a sermon series or with committee work. They are replacing church with meaningful activity that engages their communities and builds relationships, things they find missing in the church.

This says something important about the future of congregations in America. There's a growing sense that churches can't double down on the model that made them successful in 1950 in order to succeed today. To be clear, I don't think this is generational. Our respondents spanned an age range from 18 to 84. The phenomenon of people walking away from congregation-based church has much more to do with how our culture has evolved over the years for everyone, not simply for emerging adults.

Additionally, there's no reason to think that any organization can retain the same practices over a span of decades and retain its success. The most successful companies today bear very little resemblance in terms of organizational practices to the most successful organizations of a generation or two ago. Similarly, the most successful churches of the future will likely bear very little resemblance to the worship hour–dominated services that have characterized church for years.

The new expressions of faith that our dechurched respondents exhibit are akin to refugee-resettlement sites. They certainly retain much of the culture and many of the characteristics of their homeland, but they've been altered significantly by their current contexts. New forms have arisen to meet new realities, and old structures have been abandoned to meet people's present needs.

CHAPTER 4: CONVERSATION AND DOCTRINE

MEANINGFUL CONVERSATION

Think about the people you like to talk with most. What do you get out of those conversations? Do they assure you that everything you believe is right and true, or do they deepen your thinking and challenge your preconceived ideas? In the course of the conversations that you value most, does the other person drone on and on about your failings and tell you what to do, or does he or she empathize and ask questions? Do you ever talk in those conversations, or does your friend do all the talking? Do you both debate, defending your unchanging positions? Or do you collaborate and allow the information and opinions of your friend to give new shape, perspective, and life to your old ideas and problems?

I think the answers to these questions are pretty clear, at least for me. While I enjoy a good debate every now and then, the conversations I look forward to most, with old friends and new, are the ones in which we meet on an equal footing, exchange ideas, and help each other see something new about the world.

I actually just had one of these conversations last week after church. I was struggling with how to deal with a person in my life who wasn't being very kind or loving. I could see only two options: I could suffer quietly, tacitly condoning the person's harmful actions, or I could confront the person, deal with the pain and trauma that would likely ensue, and perhaps lose the relationship in the process.

My friend, who had recently been through a similar experience, helped me brainstorm alternative approaches, some of which were rooted in her experience, but many of which reflected the simple idea of trying to act as Jesus would act.

This is one of the reasons I love my church. These kinds of things happen routinely in my congregation, both with other congregants and with church leaders.

Unfortunately, our respondents reported that this sort of exchange is not what typically occurred at their churches.

CONVERSION OR CONVERSATION?

Jill was not formally interviewed for this project, but when we were discussing this subject one day, it clearly touched a nerve. "That would be me," she said. "I would be dechurched if I hadn't found my church, where we all sit around and talk."

When I asked her to elaborate, she encapsulated the feelings of so many of our respondents: "It's in relationships and conversations that I find God. It's not a real conversation if you're trying to convert me to your position. That's an argument. I'm not interested in arguing. That's not a real relationship either."

"It's in relationships and conversations that I find God."

Her comments hung in the air for some time as I struggled to make sense of what she had just said. Was it true? Are attempts at conversion inherently opposed to authentic conversation? The more I thought about it, and the more I looked into the research about communication, the more I became convinced that Jill was right.

There are a number of ways people can talk to each other. Jill was expressing a desire for authentic conversation, wherein both parties are open to being influenced by the other.

However, according to our respondents, the traditional mode of religious interaction involves one of two other models: the argumentative style, in which person A states his or her position, then person B shares his or her position, and so on, but neither party has any intention of being influenced by the other. Or the dictatorial style, in which person A speaks with the intention of influencing person B, who takes in the information without responding.

Our respondents not only articulated a strong desire for authentic conversation, but were also summarily turned off by the other two styles.

Jill's comments summarize what most of us know intuitively. The friends we find hard to keep, the relationships that are most difficult to sustain, are the ones in which an equal exchange of ideas is absent.

When I asked Chloe what she wanted out of church, she said simply, "I'm looking for people who want to have conversations with me. It's not something I need at the institutional level, although that would be great. I just want relationships."

DIALOGUE OR LECTURE?

Liam's comments supported Chloe's position. He was clear about wanting dialogue as opposed to lecture. He grew up in a Methodist church but struggled with the teachings of his home church as he got older and started reading more. He found it increasingly difficult to reconcile his new knowledge with what he considered the "anti-intellectual" stance of his congregation.

Remarkably, he was quick to point out that he wasn't looking for people to endorse his viewpoint. He just wanted authentic conversations:

> I wasn't looking for agreement. Like, I didn't need the pastor to proclaim Darwin from the pulpit like I would have done. I just wanted someone to talk to. Our old pastor never got angry or anything. He was civil. He kept me in church and could get me back. I mean, we could even discuss evolution. But with the new pastor, it was all authority and hierarchy, and that was the final straw in getting us to leave. When we couldn't talk anymore, it just wasn't worth going.

Liam has since found these conversations, but only after leaving the church. He's become much more engaged in conversations about science and faith through regular participation in various online forums. He even went so far as to say that he felt the people online were much more civil than the people he met in church.

Our respondents' resistance to the top-down conversation model wasn't simply about style or ego. They expressed a distinctly theological and spiritual rationale for wanting to have authentic conversations.

Later in our interview Liam articulated this connection very clearly:

> You know, we don't actually know. We don't have all the answers, and we don't have to. But I still come at these questions from a Christian tradition. I don't know everything, and I'm OK with that.

"We don't have all the answers, and we don't have to."

Ethan expressed similar sentiments: "There's much more mystery to God than we allow there to be or allow people to believe."

Mystery, doubt, uncertainty, questioning. For the people we talked to, these were central components of a meaningful faith, and they wanted the church to engage them in authentic conversation rather than provide predetermined, canned answers.

DEALING WITH QUESTIONS

Mark explained that understanding how a church handles questions has actually become his first screening criterion when trying out new churches:

I had a chat with a pastor at a church that I was interested in attending, and I said, "I don't want to hear about what you believe; there will be plenty of time to talk about that later. I'm not interested in seeing if we agree, because I'm sure there will be disagreement. The only question I have for you is, How do you deal with people who disagree with you? How does you church handle that? Because really, for me, that's the most important thing."

I want to be in a place that welcomes disagreement. Not to disagree to be rude or nasty, but out of legitimate differences of opinion. Being able to express those differences openly is a more authentic experience of faith to me. I think my biggest fear is that I'm going to get into another situation where I'm going to be the one asking questions, and I'm going to be shuffled out the door again. And I don't want that. I have to be able to ask questions. It's how I learn.

What I don't want is a church that says, "Yes, we love questions. In fact, here's a list of acceptable questions, and here are the acceptable answers. Does God exist? Yes. Did Jesus turn water into wine? Yes. Next question."

There's no thought or conversation, just acceptable and unacceptable questions and answers. That doesn't work for me. I question things. It's how I understand God. And I'm quite comfortable having that come back at me. I invite that difference.

"The only question I have for you is, How do you deal with people who disagree with you?"

Again and again our respondents described this combination of being comfortable with both the questioning and the uncertainty as a desirable dynamic. They felt virtually no need to resolve questions. Instead they needed a safe place to ask questions and explore possible answers, and there was a distinct feeling that this is not what church typically allows.

Emily put it succinctly when she said, "I've always had questions for the church, but there isn't much room in Christian churches and denominations to question."

When asked if they agreed with Emily that there isn't much room for questioning in church, the answer among our respondents was a resounding "Yes!" They felt the ability to ask questions and explore various aspects of their faith wasn't supported in the church, and it was a major factor in their decisions to leave.

Even when questions and conversation were courted, it was often not in a truly authentic way. As Megan told us, "They were only interested in my questions so they could answer them, and they thought they had all the answers." She felt her pastors and church leaders didn't listen to her questions because they wanted to know more about her life or because they thought she could help shape their understanding of God. Their interest in her questions was, she suspected, simply an opportunity to say what they wanted to say all along. It wasn't an authentic conversation because she had no ability to shape or influence them at all, she felt.

SHADOW MISSIONS

Our respondents also told us they'd encountered church planters, missional pastors, and on-campus religious groups who had utilized a "relationship first" model in which they were exhorted to make friends with people, gain their trust, and then invite them to church. Our respondents found these "shadow missions" abhorrent. The idea of pursuing relationships or conversations with an ulterior motive was anathema to them. They rejected the goal of shadow missions: to get people to come to God and/or the church. Our respondents preferred to simply reflect God's love to others.

Again, the dechurched value relationships and community above everything. These are the primary ways they encounter God and understand their own spirituality, develop a deeper understanding of their own faith, and put their beliefs into action. In short, they see their human relationships as an extension of their relationship with the divine. Their relationships are sacred to them—not because they replace God, but because it is in relationships that they find God.

> **They see their human relationships as an extension of their relationship with the divine.**

You can imagine their reaction, then, when pastors and church leaders tell them to forge relationships with their co-workers and acquaintances first, to build up trust, before inviting them to church. These actions, though well-intentioned, are perceived as dishonest and inauthentic.

William articulated this when he explained why he and his wife left the church:

> We wanted people to be cared for. We wanted people to have a sense that community and relationships were what really mattered. We wanted a church where growth happens organically, not where you have these thinly veiled marketing calls and evangelism under the guise of friendship.

Rather than getting to know their co-workers, neighbors, and other acquaintances so they could invite them to church, our respondents wanted to get to know them so they could love them. They wanted, Mark said, "not to change them, but to be changed by them, trusting that God will guide that process in a good way."

Aside from issues of authenticity and honesty, the other significant problem with this approach is that it automatically puts relationships on an unequal footing. Our respondents told us that the underlying message is that the person being invited to church or God is somehow less than the person extending the invitation. They said the tacit message is that there's something fundamentally wrong, broken, or, at best, not fully realized, about that person's life that can only be fixed by coming to church and being like the person doing the inviting. Our respondents viewed this as inherently judgmental and counterproductive to relationships they wanted to be built on mutual respect and authentic conversation.

Chloe, whom we met earlier, made this exact point when discussing her church's missional orientation:

> At my old church we talked a lot about being missional. And this really just meant converting people. To me, a missionary's responsibility is not to walk down the street and knock on everybody's door and try to convert them; their responsibility is to serve and to love and to form relationships. And those relationships should never be based on converting people, or telling people their belief systems are wrong or evil.

While this may seem an endorsement of a kind of humanism or universalism, very few of our respondents gave equal weight and validity to all traditions. Instead, Chloe expressed a profound trust in God as a mysterious and powerful force. She and other respondents try to respect people without abdicating their responsibility to act as God has called them to act. They're deeply reverential about people's individual stories and their diversity of experiences. But they're also leery of doctrine on the grounds that it limits, rather than clarifies, their understanding of God.

THE DIFFICULTY OF DOCTRINE

In general, the dechurched see doctrine—a set understanding of who God is, what God expects of us, and how God acts—as incompatible with relationship formation and with the rest of their lives. And, reflecting society's diminished respect for authority we discussed earlier, our respondents don't automatically respect pastors—and by extension, their doctrinal teachings—simply because they occupy the role of pastor.

Ella, a 21-year-old graduate student who had been heavily involved in campus ministry, illustrated this:

> I definitely don't always take what people tell me anymore. If the church is founded by man and men are the ones telling me how things are, then how do I know that's what God wants and not just what those men want? I do a lot more questioning now. I'm going to do it on my own either way. If the church can accept that and facilitate it, then great. I would love to go there. If it can't, then I'll move on. I'm less concerned about the particular teaching than I am about how they deal with questions.

Her comments echoed Mark's statement earlier in this chapter that he evaluated new churches on the basis of how they dealt with disagreement and questions. Ella and Mark are not only more interested in exploring the questions, mystery, and doubt that come with faith, but they also view dogma as inherently opposed to questioning and exploration.

They view dogma as inherently opposed to questioning and exploration.

Brody, a 38-year-old manager and former lay minister, expressed this same desire for a multitude of voices by referring to the priesthood of all believers:

> I think biblically, it comes through pretty clearly that we're all priests and we don't need a mediator. God is too big for one person. We need everyone to fully access God.

Jackson stated that an inability to dialogue about important issues was central to his decision to leave the church:

I wanted to think critically about my religion, and to critically challenge things. I did that very actively through my college years. I felt it strengthened my religion, but not my role in the church. The church wanted no part of that.

Ella didn't want a pastor to convince her of the theological underpinnings of church doctrine. In fact, as she and others pointed out, pastors can't convince her precisely because of their role in church leadership. Brody contended that a full understanding of God requires multiple perspectives. This understanding changes the role of the church leader from one who conveys knowledge and wisdom to one who develops and facilitates understanding. At least, that's the role the dechurched would like to see their pastors play. Furthermore, it's the only role they'll accept when choosing a pastor.

Our respondents' focus on understanding made them suspicious of doctrine. For them, doctrine creates the illusion of agreement when, in fact, universal agreement is never achievable in any organization, let alone the church.

Our respondents were well aware that people understand the same truths in myriad ways. Think about the emotions we all experience and understand as humans: love, hate, frustration, peace, happiness, comfort, and so on. We all have an understanding of these emotions, but it's unlikely that our understandings are the same. Our understanding is rooted in our experiences.

We understand love because we've experienced love, not because we read about it in a book or because someone explained it to us. We understand frustration because we've been frustrated. But it's unlikely that we've been frustrated about exactly the same things, and it's unlikely that my experience of love is the same as yours. My idea of a father is likely different from yours and even from my own dad's. This doesn't mean that any of us is wrong, of course; it simply means that we base our understanding on a combination of experiences, desires, and social expectations rather than on an objective reality.

What our respondents consistently affirmed was that basic Christian values and even what it means to be a Christian worked in the same way for them.

Cora, the 66-year-old grandmother we met earlier, described how her experiences informed and changed her understanding of God in one of the most painful ways possible. Not long before our interview, her infant grandson had died unexpectedly. It was a time of tremendous grief. The support she received from her loved ones fundamentally altered her understanding of God:

> I heard God speaking to me for the first time. I experienced his love in a wholly new way. I don't think about God in the same way anymore. It was painful, but it has deepened my understanding of the love of Christ.

Cora's experience is an example of how our understanding of God is informed by our experiences. When our experiences change, our understandings change. Sociologists call this a phenomenological approach to understanding the world.

The dechurched desire understanding, as opposed to objective knowledge, because they think a static, objective position about God and Christianity is not possible. They don't deny the existence of universal truth, however.

Joel, a former pastor, put it this way:

> As long as faith is a fundamental component of Christianity, there can never be an objective Christian position, and to pretend otherwise is just foolishness. That's the problem with presenting church as a set of rules to be learned, agreed upon, and followed. God isn't unknowable, that's not what I'm saying, but at the same time, trying to know God by distilling him down to a set of dogmatic assertions is just crazy.

Joel's distaste for dogma is based on his theology, not on reactionary individualism.

Mason, a formerly dechurched 25-year-old, explained how this theological position was fundamental in keeping him connected with his current church:

> The big emphasis is that God is making everything new. And that means you and me, too. And so a lot of different ideas and beliefs can come around the same table. I'm happy for us to go someplace new together. We don't have to agree or even end up at the exact same place. In fact, it's probably better that we don't. God is bigger than that.

The pastor at Mason's church sees himself in the role of facilitator, and Mason said that's the only reason he returned to church and it's the only reason he continues to attend. This doesn't mean that his pastor downplays the fact that he's spent more time studying and thinking about the Scriptures and Christian theology than most of his congregation, but it does mean that he doesn't deliver this knowledge to his congregation as a prepackaged set of beliefs to be either endorsed or rejected.

> He doesn't deliver this knowledge to his congregation as a prepackaged set of beliefs to be either endorsed or rejected.

Lucas, a 39-year-old, seminary-trained community developer, told us about his time working in the church as a youth director. He looked for a diverse community because he felt it leads to new and different ways to serve and know God:

> It was never easy working in the church, because I was always working against the grain. A lot of people are comfortable in homogenous units, but I'm not, or at least I don't want to be. So there was a lot of diversity and community engagement in what we were doing with the youth program. And that's hard for a lot of people, but I can't really access God or bring God to others in a forum where we all agree already. Like, what am I adding to that?

Doctrine and dogma—the view that to be a Christian and do Christianity you must first adhere to all the things Christians agree to—are incompatible with the way the dechurched see God working in their own lives and in the world around them.

DIFFERENCES IN COMMUNITY

The church's focus on doctrine and dogma is also perceived as counterproductive to the high value our respondents place on community. Mark explained his view that the church has chosen to focus on dogma to the detriment of community formation.

> That ability to create community is the biggest thing the church has lost because of the boundaries the church has put in and the barriers with dogma and statements of faith. They've lost what it means to be a community. Communities have differences of opinion. We're individuals, so, yeah, we're going to have differences of opinion. We're not a community *in spite* of our differences; we're a community *because* we're different. Because we bring different things to the table. That's what brings us together. Whereas the church seems to take this position that what brings us together is our commonality.

The dechurched aren't looking for a church in which they agree with everyone. In fact, they invite differences of opinion. This is at the heart of how they understand Jesus. A church that wants to be a home to the dechurched (or those about to be done with church) should start figuring out how to facilitate productive conversations between people with varying viewpoints.

They invite differences of opinion. This is at the heart of how they understand Jesus.

Later in his interview, Mark told us what we heard in other forms from so many of our respondents: "So that's what I'm looking for. I'm looking for someone to say, 'Yeah, you're different from us. That's what we want. Come join us.'"

Another respondent put it this way:

> Not only am I not interested in agreement, but I want to invite difference, because as soon as you have agreement, you have people on the outside. I've been on the outside, and that's no way to have a community.

These comments drive home the point our respondents made about the way difference creates community. We've all been on the outside at some time in our lives. That's even happened to a great many people in church, and this seems counter to their understanding of Christianity because it's counter to their understanding of community. Once I understood how the dechurched made this connection between their faith and their community, their desire for conversation and dislike of doctrine and dogma became understandable.

Allison echoed these sentiments when she described her ideal version of church. The only kind of church that could get her back, she said, is "a church where everyone is welcome as they are and there are many different voices coming from the pulpit."

Rather than courting and creating this kind of diversity, the church, in our respondents' view, strives for uniformity and conformity. And because uniformity is not achievable, they viewed the church as fostering an inauthentic environment in which they felt they could never share their full selves, a theme we'll explore in Chapter 5.

RECONCILING THE NEED FOR DOCTRINE AND AUTHENTIC CONVERSATION

This part of the project, around issues of conversation and dogma, left Ashleigh and me feeling sympathetic to both our respondents, who felt stymied in their efforts to understand and explore their faith, and to religious professionals, most of whom go into the profession because they feel a calling to share their understanding of God with others.

We had countless conversations about the difficulties pastors must face in dealing with questions they had already faithfully considered and answered for themselves years ago. How does a pastor in that situation engage in the conversation without making it seem as if his or her faith is up for grabs or on shaky ground? What kinds of conversation do the dechurched want? How can productive experiences be facilitated to keep fewer people from being done and maybe even to reengage some of those who have left?

Toward the end of this chapter, we'll explore ways to facilitate these conversations without abdicating adherence to fundamental theological tenets or creating uncertainty around theological absolutes.

A THEOLOGY OF COLLECTIVE DIFFERENCE

It would be a mistake to conclude that the dechurched desire an individualistic theology. Instead, they desire to form a theology based on conversation and difference as opposed to dictation and dogma. It's not individualistic in a "do it yourself" sense but rather an act of community in a "do it ourselves" sense.

As a longtime churchgoer and academic observer of Christianity and new Christian movements, I was struck by how robust and developed the theological presence and defense of diversity were among our respondents. When I finally sat down to analyze all of these stories about the importance of diversity, I expected to hear a lot of complaints about church rules. And I wasn't inclined to be especially sympathetic personally or academically to that position. It seems inconsistent to me to proclaim an affinity for a faith but then to pick and choose which of its tenets to hold.

What emerged from these interviews, however, was a clearly argued and carefully considered theological position. Nothing we could see in the interviews amounted to rejection of difficult church teachings or biblical passages. Instead, we encountered a thoughtful and impassioned theology born of our respondents' preference for diversity and difference built on authentic relationship as opposed to agreement.

These theological positions actually fly in the face of a lot of contemporary research. Our respondents consistently told a story different from much of what other academics have been uncovering. Our respondents didn't desire a God who serves them or a religious system that allows them more freedom and affirmation. Instead, they were seeking and defending an understanding of God that comes through interactions with others in a sustained and intentional way, and they didn't object when this understanding constrained and restricted their own behavior or made them uncomfortable.

CREATING NEW MODELS

For so many of our respondents, it was a process to leave the church. Many of the dechurched tell the same kind of story about gradually disengaging from official church structures. Some tried to reform their congregations. Others told about finding a small space inside the church structure where they could focus on relationships and cultivate diversity. Small groups, Bible studies, and alternative worship services on Sunday or Wednesday nights often filled this purpose for a time. They were still connected to the church, but through lack of leadership, time, or concern, they were left outside of the attention paid to regular Sunday worship and other collective experiences.

This phase could be short or take months or even years. In fact, several people we would consider dechurched are *still* officially connected to the church through these groups even though they haven't attended church or tithed in years. For many, however, these groups and activities were a part of the process of disengagement. Once they stepped away from corporate worship and the influence of church leadership, they had no need or desire for those old experiences.

We asked Jason, whom we met in Chapter 3, what he's doing now that he's left the church. He's still regularly involved in fellowship, and he expresses great satisfaction with how that's structured: Each week they get together over a Sunday morning meal to plan activities for the coming week. They often read Scripture and pray, but not always.

When asked to identify the source of his satisfaction with this new model and why it's so different from other expressions of church, he said:

> My wife and I are completely open to people's spiritual journeys even though a lot of them are very different from ours. That's the big difference. *We no longer stand on the ground of religious doctrine; we stand on the ground of relationship.* That's really what we have in common now with the people we worship with. (Emphasis added.)

This is quite a big step for Jason considering his long history of active leadership in churches, but he's not alone.

Cole, the church school superintendent we met earlier, expressed a similar sentiment:

> I didn't want to be part of the machine anymore. I wanted to change the focus of my life to relationships, and I just couldn't see a way for that to happen inside the institutional church.

Jason's and Cole's comments underscore their belief that they understand their relationship with God through their relationships with people. Their foundation is relationships, not the statements of belief handed down by learned theologians or pastors that had guided the majority of their religious lives.

RELIGIOUS INDIVIDUALISM

In the 1980s religious practitioners and academics alike were concerned about growing religious individualism in America. Robert Bellah's *Habits of the Heart*, first published in 1985, profiled Sheila, a woman who had constructed her own syncretic religion which drew from a number of spiritual sources. She referred to it as "Sheilaism." It was very much an individual form of religion.

One implication of individualized religion is that, just as there are no two Sheilas, there can be no truly collective form of adherents to Sheilaism. The belief system lived and died with Sheila alone. Sociologists understood that if this were to become more popular it would have widespread implications for society. One of the primary functions of religion has always been to bring people together to affirm common values through collective ritual. Sheilaism would negate all of that value. Religious practitioners, of all faiths, wondered what role pastors and churches would play in an era dominated by individualistic, DIY religion. They also fretted over the relativism present in Sheilaism and the lack of commitment to objective truth found in God. These are understandable concerns, and, to a certain extent, they remain issues to the present day.

Even though a wave of individualized religion hasn't yet fully presented itself, traces of it still run throughout our society. In fact, this concept presented itself again in a different form in the research for *Soul Searching* by Christian Smith and Melinda Lundquist Denton. In this book, the authors argue that what best characterizes the faith of American teenagers is a kind of moralistic therapeutic deism (MTD). Their study, based on thousands of interviews with American teenagers, concludes that teens believe in a God that exists, wants people to be nice to each other, and answers prayers in times of trouble; that life is generally meant for enjoyment and happiness; and that good people go to heaven when they die.

This research touched the same chord among pastors that *Habits of the Heart* had decades earlier. But just as these impulses have always been present in our highly individualized society, our research shows a substantial undercurrent of people who take a position quite different from either this individualized approach or the corporatized approach that characterizes so much organized religious activity today. It is, in many respects, a third way and moves beyond issues of individuality and conformity.

A THIRD WAY

What we see in the stories throughout this book is a continual emphasis on reaffirming the collective. In many ways, Jason's story is a perfect illustration of this point. After trying to reform the church to bend more toward community, he left, but he and his wife took two things with them: God and a commitment to community. The dechurched are more interested in the group than the individual, but they bristle at the notion that unity means uniformity.

Early in the life of this book I had the opportunity to present some of our findings at the Future of the Church conference that Group Publishing hosts every year. The response was tremendous, but it was a connection with one of the other speakers that truly drove this point home for me.

Danny Cortez, the Southern Baptist Convention pastor whose congregation had garnered much media attention earlier in the year for adopting a "third way" approach to homosexuality, was on a panel about homosexuality and the church. As he explained the third way—an explicit attempt to live in tension and disagreement as a congregation about the issue of homosexuality—it occurred to me that this was exactly what my respondents had been trying to describe when they discussed dogma and conversation. Regardless of its value with respect to the issue of homosexuality, the desire to put unity first and disagreement second while not glossing over or hiding disagreement was precisely what my respondents had been explaining to me throughout this project.

The following statements from people who left the church and formed small, regular fellowship communities illustrate this:

> Any agenda is really hard for me to get behind. Somebody is going to be in charge; then somebody has to decide who is in and who is out. I still feel very reactive to that...What clues do we have about who Jesus was and what he wanted? Well, he walked around, he collected people, he lived in community with a dozen people, he talked about God, he blew up religious systems, he confronted political injustice, and then he died. When I started thinking about leaving the church, it was because I was like, "OK, so how do we respond to that call from Jesus?" So as I sifted through the values I saw there, I realized what mattered—what I think matters to God—is relationship, friendship, and true spirituality. What corrupts that is organizing it through an agenda like collecting money or building buildings. I think my best guess of what Jesus would have wanted would have been small groups of people to meet in homes and be friends, help each other, and serve the poor. End of story.
>
> — Isabella

I can't imagine a church I would come back to right now because it would be a system, and I wouldn't want to be in a system... I think it works to have meals together, go to movies together, and talk about what's going on, but if it's formal, and if there's one person in charge, just shoot me.

—William

It seems no matter what church it is, there's always going to be a sense of "Well, we're right, and other people are wrong" at the end of the day. We're just not really interested in that. We miss the community, but we're finding that in other places among people who are in similar places as us. We interact on the Internet, and some of them are popping up in physical places, too.

—Liam

What emerged among our respondents is an insistence that the church doesn't have a people problem. In all cases, our respondents asked for *more* interactions with all people, including Christians, not fewer.

What the dechurched say is needed, and what they've created both practically and theologically after leaving the church, is an organization that's better for them.

In order to reengage the dechurched, then, our respondents are clear that the church needs to adopt policies and practices that disseminate power, reduce the role of the pastor as the holder and conveyor of all knowledge, and utilize organizational resources to empower people rather than to control them.

ORGANIZATIONAL INEVITABILITIES

So how can this desire for authentic conversation be implemented in a congregation? Is it even possible, or is it simply a clamoring for something different, even if that something is unsustainable?

The answer to these questions may lie outside the immediate realm of religious organizations. When we look to the existing research about the impact organizational structures have on organizational activity, we can begin to piece together a strategy that allows for a more engaged, participative congregation without undermining the power of organizational structure.

Existing research suggests that in any bureaucracy, power tends to become centralized, innovation is gradually diminished, and routines become cemented as the organization grows or simply continues to exist over time. The nature of the modern bureaucracy is to erase individual desire. In order to resist those forces, organizational leaders must be intentional and strategic. It's not enough to simply wish for things to be participative and innovative.

How many pastors have lamented the slow pace of change in their own congregations? Even founding pastors often find that after only a few short months or years of doing church, they've largely lost the ability to move the congregation in a new direction.

This is true of all modern organizations, not just churches. It's the nature of bureaucracies, not a function of poor leadership, bad vision, a sign of the withdrawal of God's grace, or unfaithful followers. It's simply a part of living in the modern world.[1]

In fact, the power of organizational structure is so great that even in organizations of as few as 25 people, there's evidence that the organization's vision or mission statement has virtually no impact on day-to-day operations. A church can strive valiantly to be participatory or missional, but if it retains a centralized leadership structure that controls money, time, and other resources, the church will never achieve that vision.

THE POWER OF EXPECTATION

The primary force determining the level of participation in any environment is expectation. For example, when we walk into Target, we expect there to be organized shelves of products for sale and people who are working to help us complete our purchases. We aren't expecting to walk in and make the things we want from scratch. People aren't sewing clothes at Target. People aren't making their own lawn furniture. And the people working there would never expect their customers to act that way. Imagine how bizarre it would be if someone walked into a Target and started building his own toaster.

On the other hand, think of our homes. I don't even want to think about the "conversation" my wife and I would have if I walked in the door of my house and treated it like a Target, expecting everything to be done and made for me, ready to consume. Home isn't solely a place of consumption; it's a production site as well. If we want food, we have

---

[1] For more information, see *The New Institutionalism in Organizational Analysis* by Walter W. Powell and Paul J. DiMaggio.

to make it. If something breaks, we fix it. If we want a room painted, we paint it. Our organizational resources at home are configured much more differently than organizational resources are at Target, and these configurations help to shape our expectations.

Well, what kind of organizational expectations do we have of our churches? Are they set up more like Target or like home? Do our churches produce a product to be consumed, or are they sites where the people who walk in the door are themselves producers and makers?

Additionally, people bring their own expectations when they walk into church, and organizational resources are often allocated to meet those expectations. It's hard to do church differently when people already have an idea of what church should look like.

For example, I recently worked with a pastor and leadership team that couldn't figure out why they were having such a hard time getting people to do things other than attend worship services on Sunday mornings. They concluded, "People are just too busy to do anything." "Nobody really cares that much." "They say they want things, but they don't want to have to do any of it." The sociologist in me has always bristled at these arguments, because they focus on personal motivations while ignoring the importance of structure.

So I asked a simple question: "What's the main thing you do right now?" The answer was a Sunday morning worship service. They were all proud of that service, how creative it was and how well it went. Then, just as I suggested you do in Chapter 3, I asked them to estimate how many hours went into the Sunday service, including sermon preparation, volunteer hours, band practice, morning host and setup committees, planning meetings, and Sunday school. They calculated they spent over 100 hours each week on their worship service.

But my point was different from the one I made in Chapter 3. I asked, "What's second? What in your church gets the second most hours, and what's that total?" After much initial disagreement, they eventually decided their small groups were second, and the total number of staff and volunteer hours that went into coordinating and hosting them was fewer than 30 each week. Two things were significant to me: (1) They devoted far fewer of their resources to the second activity on their list, and (2) there was immediate agreement that the 90-minute worship service was the church's first priority but widespread disagreement about what came next.

Is it any wonder, then, that people walk in the door with the idea that church is a place that provides services for them? It's the expectation that has been established before they walk in the door and the one that most churches cultivate weekly. Given this reality, should it really be surprising that they expect the church to provide the same level of service, organization, and coordination for every other activity in which the church is engaged?

Just by asking a couple of key questions, we were able to see that people weren't, in fact, too busy, apathetic, or lazy. Instead, the organization had set up and fulfilled an expectation. The church acted like Target, and the congregants behaved like customers. Just as it would be unthinkable to make something in a Target, the church had made it unthinkable for congregants to make anything in their church.

If the leadership team truly wanted people to be more participatory, the church needed to be more like home, where everyone is expected to contribute.

And this is precisely what the dechurched want.

REACHING THE DONES

I would never suggest turning your entire organization upside down to accommodate the dechurched. In so doing, you'd inevitably run off all of those people who come to church with the expectation that there will be a service they can consume and digest through the rest of their week. Those people are truly valuable to the church, and that should not be understated or obscured.

But if you care about the dechurched, then make part of your structure function more like home. Support it with time, money, and other institutional resources, and don't try to package it or control it.

These two organizational impulses can coexist. As we've seen throughout this chapter, the dechurched desire a place where real, authentic conversation occurs. Think about ways to facilitate those conversations.

- Use church resources to bring speakers in to facilitate discussion.

- Have a talk-back session at the end of every service in which whoever delivered the sermon is available to answer questions and talk about the day's message.

- There's no need to actively court controversy, but give congregants, rather than your leadership team, the power to select speakers, and trust God to be at work in the process.

- Find the people in your church who would most desire conversation, and support them in organizing a participatory worship service once a month with more dialogue than sermon.

- Facilitate meals in people's homes by using church funds to hire babysitters or provide food.

I'm sure you can think of many more ways to encourage authentic conversation within your church. Just remember the goal: to support participation, not to provide another service to be consumed. For the dechurched, and for those who are on their way out, church needs to be more like home and less like Target.

CHAPTER 5: MEANINGFUL MINISTRY AND MORAL PRESCRIPTION

THE CHURCH'S MORAL TEACHINGS

The final theme that emerged as we explored common reasons for leaving the church is the disconnect our respondents felt between engaging the world meaningfully and the moral prescriptions of the church. There's a strong sentiment among the Dones that the church is more interested in policing morality than working to counteract entrenched structural barriers, especially with regard to poverty. This sentiment was tied to the Dones' sensitivity to perceptions of Christians as hypocritical and unconcerned with the world and was increasingly incongruent with the lives our respondents were living outside the church walls.

In particular, our respondents felt the church thinks of morality only in terms of behavior regulation (primarily with regard to sex and substances) to the exclusion of economic issues. Our respondents were unanimously more interested in bringing Jesus to the world around them.

As Aaron told me, "They were moral police: drugs and sex, drugs and sex, drugs and sex. That's it. I wanted to deal with poverty. They just wanted to police me."

Aaron's understanding of this issue is particularly illustrative. He directly interpreted the church's admonition against sexual immorality and drug use as an attempt to control him. Aaron didn't attribute church teachings about drugs and sex to a concern for him as a person or as an expression of God's desire for his life. Rather than stemming from love, he believed the church's teachings were an expression of control, power, and authority.

This is another illustration of the Dones' skepticism toward religious leaders. They simply aren't predisposed to think that church leaders have their best interests at heart. Whether Aaron's interpretation is right or wrong, it's important to acknowledge that his interpretation exists and was echoed repeatedly by our other respondents. In the minds of Aaron and other dechurched people, then, a lack of action outside of the walls of the church is coupled with a belief that the church is mostly interested in controlling people rather than helping them.

With that backdrop, the conversations we had with the dechurched about the common good and community make a lot more sense and can be understood as more than just anger at the church for telling them what to do. In fact, none of our respondents questioned God's authority to govern their morality or rejected organized religion because they couldn't find a pastor or church that would condone their behaviors and lifestyles.

None of our respondents left the church because they wanted to drink alcohol and the church taught against it. None of our respondents left because they were living with a partner while their pastors preached about the sanctity of marriage. A couple of our respondents who identified as homosexual did tell us they left because of issues surrounding sexual behavior and homosexuality. But what drove the vast majority away was their perception that the church focuses on issues of personal morality exclusively or predominantly while ignoring what our respondents felt were much bigger issues.

To our respondents, preaching a message about the evils of drinking seemed like so much small change compared to big-ticket items such as poverty, racism, and gender inequality.

> **Preaching a message about the evils of drinking seemed like so much small change compared to big-ticket items such as poverty, racism, and gender inequality.**

WORDS AND DEEDS

As news about racial unrest in Ferguson, Missouri, was making daily headlines, Diane told us, "I'm very interested in how the faith community is or isn't actively contributing—other than yackety-yak from the pulpit—

to the conversation about racism and police brutality right now." Diane had a long history in the church and affirmed throughout her interview that there's value in the message coming from the pulpit but only if it's backed up with action. She didn't question the authority of the pastor to take moral stances and guide the ethics of a congregation, but she longed for these to be combined with loving action addressing big issues. She frequently referenced James 2:26: "Faith without deeds is dead."

In addition to these issues regarding the focus of moral teachings, there was broad feeling among our respondents that the teachings of church leaders actually resulted in very little impact.

Jeff is a former megachurch pastor who was overseeing digital ministry for a congregation that numbered into the thousands on a given week. He had a long history of working in the church and had reached a point where he was well paid, respected, and influential. Eventually, though, he began to question what kind of an impact his congregation was actually having. The tipping point for him came late one evening after a small group had spent a long time talking about how to respond to a group member who was dating two women at the same time:

> On the way home, I just couldn't get over the absurdity of that conversation. I mean, I don't want to condone his actions, as they were clearly destructive relationally, but I knew he wasn't going to change, not in his heart, and I think everyone else there knew it, too. We were just focused on making his behavior conform, thinking his heart would follow. But that's just not how it works. I started putting all of these pieces together, and I left my job and the church when I realized that we as evangelicals were doing lots of lifestyle indoctrination and very little soul transformation.

Jeff felt the church's moral teachings were only scratching the surface of what it means to be a Christian. There can be a rule for everything, and a person can follow those rules, according to Jeff, without having a heart that's truly reflective of Jesus. For Jeff, the problem was that God had been reduced to a series of guidelines to be followed rather than a general orientation of the soul.

Mary took this sentiment a step further when she told us, "The church kept getting in the way of my relationship with God with all of their arbitrary legalism…so I left." The key word here is *arbitrary*. Mary not only found the church's moral teachings unhelpful, but she also couldn't find consistent theological underpinnings in the enforcement of some norms and rules and not others.

She asked, "Why do we get so hung up on just a few things? Like, tell me how ignoring the poor is *not* a moral failure? Why don't pastors ever have to resign for that?"

Mary's accusation summarized what is most significant about the stance the dechurched take with regard to moral issues. If they were simply frustrated and unfulfilled by the dos and don'ts coming from the pulpit, this wouldn't be noteworthy. Numerous polls and studies have confirmed that we're witnessing a general shift in our society as more and more people tell us they find church teachings about morality unhelpful, ineffective, or both. Tossing the dechurched into that category would hardly be worth noting.

However, the dechurched aren't fed up with the moral teachings of the church, nor do they question, like so many others, the authority of pastors to play such a role. Instead, they're irritated and driven away because of their perception that the church focuses on lifestyle while ignoring deep issues that tear communities apart.

It's understandable, in the context of this book, that they would be so concerned about their communities. As we've seen throughout these pages, they take a distinctly biblical approach to community as a way to access and understand God. Repairing and healing these divisions, then, is not driven by a political agenda. In fact, our sample wasn't skewed by an over-representation of the religiously conservative or the religiously liberal.

The dechurched long to show Jesus to as many people as possible and, in the process, deepen others' understanding of God. The Dones are concerned that the church's narrow focus on morality to the exclusion of other issues not only obscures the full teachings of Jesus for others, but actually limits their own access to God.

This is part of what makes the Dones unique. For them, the church's concentration on moral policing allows it to escape what they view as the church's responsibility to devote meaningful resources to addressing systemic, root causes of unfairness. They feel that the church's moral posture allows it to pay lip service to action through calls for better behavior while keeping the bulk of the church's resources inside the church. While they wouldn't advocate abandoning moral principles in any way, they do think these principles should be coupled with an "outside of the walls" approach to ministry.

Ella gave us the following snapshot of this point of view:

> I went to church because I thought I could do some good there that I couldn't do alone, not to come home angry because they said my friends would burn in hell for who they loved while they debated how much money to spend on the new church parking lot.

Ella's statement reveals several important beliefs. First, she believes in the power of Christians to act together to do good in the world, and she doesn't believe she can do it by herself. Ella, and many like her, long for the church to be a place of coordinated action that impacts the local community.

Second, the dechurched have a very sensitive meter for what they consider organizational hypocrisy. Ella viewed the message condemning her gay friends combined with a request for money to build a parking lot as a series of coordinated and interlocking organizational activities. For Ella, raising money for a new parking lot meant not spending money to help feed the poor or address other social issues. Although Ella was quick to point out that she didn't think these things were intentionally coordinated, she felt the end result was just as powerful as if they were.

She went on to explain in detail the inner tension she experienced. She said it became more and more difficult to explain to her gay and lesbian friends, and to herself, how she could stay in a church that was condemning them to eternal suffering and agony. For a long time, she was able to justify her decision to stay because her church was engaged in a number of community-service and neighborhood-advocacy efforts. However, that changed when a new pastor, determined to grow the church, came on board. At the same time, the youth director, who was spearheading the local missions effort, left. The turn inward, to focus on the church building and membership, was solidified around the parking lot, which was going to cost tens of thousands of dollars.

At this point, the math no longer made sense for her. She was alienating her friends and increasingly conflicted about being in a place that opposed her own beliefs. And now she had lost the opportunity to reflect Jesus' compassion to those outside the walls of the church. The parking lot simply became symbolic of an inward focus that she felt was inconsistent with her understanding of a God who cares about everyone. To be clear, and as is illustrated by the fact that she stuck around for so long, Ella wasn't advocating that the church abandon the parking lot or give up its internal ministry. She simply wanted those efforts to be coupled with activities outside of the church.

Ella's story illustrates how much importance the dechurched place on action. Keep in mind that while Ella eventually ended up leaving, she was willing to jeopardize her friendships outside the church and wrestle with the cognitive dissonance of attending a church that seemed to present a uniform message counter to her own beliefs just so she could remain engaged in the things the church was doing in the community.

In other words, she took great social and personal risk to remain attached to a structure that afforded her the opportunity to do the work of God.

When Ella moved, she tried to find a new church but encountered more of the same.

> I was kind of hoping to find a place where folks could be accepting and actually do something and not just be the people who collect money and pay bills and "Alright, here's your sermon for the week; you can go home." Like that's enough.

After looking at five or six different churches, she couldn't find anything. So now she spends her weekends volunteering with Habitat for Humanity.

She misses the community aspect of church, though, saying, "It's just kind of a gap in my life. I wish for more community." But she's quick to point out that she doesn't feel the need for more organized religion. "My best religious experiences have been when we're just outside, doing Bible study, sitting in the grass, sharing life together."

What she wanted, and what nearly all of our respondents wanted, was for the church to leverage its organizational resources and infrastructure to get more things done outside of the church walls and to build community. Again, our respondents weren't done with church because they disagreed with their churches' theology or because they disliked the people. These are the reasons people switch churches. People opt out of organized religion altogether because they think the structure is fundamentally flawed.

THE CHURCH'S TEACHING ON HOMOSEXUALITY

As our respondents described their frustrations with the church's moral teachings, the issue of homosexuality came up frequently. While we expected to hear that people who identified as gay or lesbian left the church because they felt personally persecuted, these stories were rare. Instead, we heard from a lot of straight people who felt they couldn't continue to reconcile their relationships with gay friends with the teachings of the church, especially when they felt there were larger conversations the church should be having.

During an interview in a coffee shop, a friend of the person I was talking to stopped by because she'd overheard our conversation, which had hit on the topic of homosexuality. She apologized for interrupting and asked, "Can we, as a church, just get everything else right—love you're neighbor, feed the poor, all that stuff—and *then* talk about homosexuality? Can we just move that conversation to the bottom of the evangelical priority list?"

Her questions became the seed for how I posed this issue in future interviews when the topic came up, and the agreement with this sentiment was overwhelming. Respondents felt that spending so much time dealing with homosexuality wasn't in the best interest of the church and was actually distracting from what many saw as its larger mission. Our respondents didn't necessarily disagree with conservative church views of homosexuality, but they found the issue to be relatively minor compared to the amount of division and distraction it created.

> Our respondents didn't necessarily disagree with conservative church views of homosexuality, but they found the issue to be relatively minor compared to the amount of division and distraction it created.

When the issue of homosexuality came up in Ethan's interview, he said:

> When I finally stepped away from the church, I got this macro view, and I started associating with people who didn't go to church. Then it was like, "No wonder I wasn't turning people to God when I was bashing gay people and calling them sinners." So I was able to take myself out of that and was able to understand them and the hang-up they have with Christians.

Ethan's views about homosexuality didn't change when he left, but his focus on the issue did. It was, he decided, just not a productive conversation and not worth having when there were so many other areas of agreement and unity.

THE DESIRE FOR ACTION

As we mention throughout this book, the dechurched are doers.

Take 29-year-old Marcus, for example. He told us, "I decided I wanted to *do* things, not *be* things, and that wasn't happening in the church. So I left."

At age 70, Diane told us nearly the same thing. "There are too many words spoken in church, and too little action in society. I'm done with that."

Both Marcus and Diane want their identities to be formed by their actions.

Aubrey is a 35-year-old technician with a doctorate and is no longer involved in a religious community. She was heavily involved when she was younger, however, and her story illustrates the general theme that, among the dechurched, community action trumps belief:

> I'm very much about my neighbor next door to me. I think one of the reasons I joined that church is simply because my friends were there and they were doing things. It just got to the point where it was something to do on Thursday nights. You'd sing, there'd be a speaker, then you'd sing some more. They'd tell you about events and ways to be involved in the community; there were retreats and gatherings. I felt it was a safe environment for me, and it was. I still have some very good friends from that experience. In terms of the belief, though, it was not for me, but that part didn't matter as much.

Theological agreement, especially with regard to moral issues, was simply not as important to Aubrey as being a part of a community of action. She eventually left organized religion when she outgrew the college ministry she described above and couldn't find a replacement with a similar focus, but she never stopped doing things in her local community.

Earlier we heard from Diane, the 70-year-old former pastor with a master's degree in divinity. She spent a lifetime working on issues such as migrant rights, gender equality, and economic justice at both the local and national levels. She explained the relationship between community, belief, and action as she recounted why she left the church late in life:

> Why am I done? As an older woman, I don't find community in the church, especially because my friends have moved on to other, more relevant communities, or have themselves become Dones. I don't have my faith nurtured by the words,

don't like being preached at, and frankly, just don't believe in the institution anymore as a force for good in the world. Even before I went to seminary, I questioned much of the church but felt I could do more good by working within the system than by throwing rotten tomatoes at it. And I did work within the system for decades to try to help bring about social justice on an institutional level. But I was just one person and eventually got tired of butting my head against the wall. I found I did much more good and lived out my faith working with and for the disenfranchised outside the walls of the church.

When pressed to explain what kind of walls she was butting her head against, Diane said it was always issues of belief as the church tried to figure out where it stood on some particular issue. Diane found those conversations useful and necessary to a certain extent but grew tired when she concluded that those conversations seemed to be nearly all her church was doing. In fact, on the religious fundamentalism scale mentioned earlier, Diane emerged as relatively conservative theologically. She didn't want her church to give up its moral prescriptions, but she also wanted it to do the work of Jesus by showing love to "the least of these" in society.

She found that when she worked outside the walls of the church, she was able to do simple things that were undeniably good, in a community of people who were doing similar work with similar hearts. As she said, she's a doer, and it meant more to her to act boldly than to believe uniformly. Of course, both are possible, but in her experience, it was far more likely for bold action to take place outside the church.

Again and again, our respondents told us that, except on an extremely small number of issues, they don't see the world in terms of black and white. They were much more interested in the gray spaces between their certainties. Furthermore, they were unconcerned about ensuring that those around them view the world as they do. To them, this was a more honest and authentic expression of faith.

They thought the idea of uniformity of belief first and action second was a way to avoid action altogether, because, they felt, there will never be uniformity of belief or conformity of behavior. They said they've sat through numerous church services in which they disagreed with the message. They've worked for decades in the church and have counseled people who were struggling with their questions about God. They've been in countless conversations with people they respected and loved who held fundamentally different positions from each other and from the churches they belonged to. In the end, they realized that none of these things—neither the doubt, nor the questions, nor the disagreement—should preclude them from acting together on behalf of God.

> **In the end, they realized that none of these things—neither the doubt, nor the questions, nor the disagreement—should preclude them from acting together on behalf of God.**

It became clear that the dechurched are simply looking for people who are also striving for common ground. They're done with being involved in a structure that focuses on what they view as a narrow and unattainable moral conformity to the exclusion of showing love, grace, and forgiveness to those outside of walls of the church. They believe these forces compel the church inward rather than outward, and that is clearly at odds with what the dechurched desire.

Aspects of this sentiment are explored in depth in Chapter 3. The organizational barriers described in that chapter are frustrating, in part, because the Dones understand the potential impact of bringing the message of Jesus to the world.

Again, this desire exists apart from theological orientation. If the Dones were simply interested in advancing a particular theological position, they would have simply moved to churches more in tune with their own liberal or conservative understandings of Christianity.

Instead, the dechurched are leaving regardless of theological belief, and have no qualms about being a part of communities in which people disagree. What they insist upon is sharing the transformational message of Christianity in practical, meaningful ways.

CHAPTER 6:
BEING THE CHURCH NO ONE WANTS TO LEAVE

LUCK

I wrote the bulk of this book in a coffee shop and in the process made what my wife calls my "coffee shop friends." We know each other only because we happen to stop by the same coffee shop at the same times of the week. And we're bound by our resentment of nonregulars who occasionally come in and take our seats.

One day, one of these friends, Julie, asked me what I was writing. As I explained the project, she held her thumb and index finger about an inch apart and said, "Oh, man, I totally get it. I think I'm this close to being dechurched."

When I asked her why she was still attending and why she was thinking about leaving, she told me a story about a projector. "In my two years at my church, we've really done only a couple of things. We went caroling for Christmas to invite people to the Christmas services, and we raised money for a projector to use in our worship services. And I was involved in both of those efforts, because I really, really care about my church."

"Well those don't seem like terrible things," I said. "What's wrong with them?"

"No," she explained, "they aren't terrible things, but they aren't really *things* either. I was a new Christian when I came to this church, but now that I've gotten a better understanding of what Jesus wants for us, I really want to put that understanding into action."

"OK," I said, "I think that makes a lot of sense, but how does leaving your church help that process?"

"You know, it probably doesn't. I mean, I would really like to stay. I'm further along my journey than I was before I got here, but I still need help, and these people have been great to me. I don't really want to go and do it alone, but doing it alone is better than doing nothing."

There's one more part of her story I want to tell, but let's hang out here for just a moment. There are a number of ideas encapsulated in this brief conversation that are worth understanding better. Like the refugee, Julie doesn't want to leave. She wants to remain right where she is, in her home church, with people who have been good to her. But the central component of her faith is action. Unlike many of the people who were formally interviewed for this project, she doesn't yet feel equipped to step out confidently on her own. She lacks the training, knowledge, and, most important, the community outside of her church to make that transition.

In Julie's story, we see nearly all of the warning signs of someone who's thinking about leaving organized religion. She feels stymied by the organization, sensing that it no longer works to further her relationship with God and the life she feels Jesus wants her to live.

So what can the church do for her? What *should* the church do for her? The rest of my conversation with Julie may shed some light on possible answers.

"Well why haven't you left then?" I asked.

"You know, I don't know. I do know that it was helpful to talk to my pastor. Luckily I know my pastor pretty well, so when I told him I thought we should do more stuff, he agreed, and he let me form a group that does outreach and volunteering on a regular basis."

Julie went on to explain some of the plans she had for the group. Though they hadn't done their first project yet, other people had expressed interest, and she was excited. Perhaps this church would continue to be a viable option for her after all.

There are two ways, I think, to understand Julie's experience. On one hand, this is an example of a pastor who made a really great decision and worked to empower his congregant. A new Christian comes to church, is discipled, and then becomes empowered by the blessing of the pastor to go and live out her faith in the world. This is a success story, one that could be heralded in seminaries and Bible colleges to show how pastors can empower and disciple people in their churches. Most pastors care deeply about their congregants' spiritual development and want them to be fulfilled and constantly deepening their relationship with God. In many ways, then, this cautionary tale of Julie, the congregant who almost got away, places the pastor in the central role as hero. If he hadn't acted as he did, Julie might well have left. The conclusion here is inescapable: Pastors should act more like Julie's.

But there's another way to understand Julie's story, one that's more consistent with the rest of the data in this book. Think for a moment about Julie's words: "Luckily I know my pastor pretty well…and he let me form a group…"

Julie used the word *luck*. Do we really want luck to be the thing standing between Julie and the door? While Julie's pastor undoubtedly did the right thing from the perspective of keeping Julie from becoming dechurched, his decision seems to be based on the fact that he knew Julie pretty well so he did something he may not have otherwise done. Indeed, the lack of this kind of activity in Julie's two-year experience with the church is proof of this claim. Additionally, it's clear that the power to make this kind of decision in Julie's church rested firmly with the pastor. When I pressed her on these issues, she confirmed that that was the case.

So Julie was fortunate that she found an outlet for her energies and desires, and the church was fortunate that she didn't walk out the door. It could have just as easily gone the other way.

What if her pastor had been having a bad day when she approached him? What if her pastor had a weak moment of pride or ego and quashed Julie's idea out of jealousy or embarrassment? What if, instead of knowing Julie really well, the pastor only vaguely knew of Julie, or what if he didn't know her at all? Pastors are busy. Running a church is hard work. It's not always possible to know everyone. What if, at the pastor's previous church, people had been allowed to start a group on their own and one of the organizers put forth theological ideas that weren't in line with the teachings of the church? I would imagine this would have left her pastor with a distaste for starting groups that he couldn't directly control.

If any of these dynamics had been present, would Julie's pastor still have let her start an outreach ministry?

This understanding of Julie's story calls for a different kind of solution. No amount of training can eliminate weak moments, enable pastors to be connected to all of their congregants, or undo the power of a bad personal experience. The solution that Julie's story demands is organizational. If well-meaning pastors operated with better organizational structures and strategies, then the church's ability to retain its most committed believers wouldn't come down to luck. The solution needed is a structural one, not a personal one.

SAME FAITH, NEW CONTEXTS

Nearly every pastor I've ever spoken with has expressed a desire to empower congregants. Some clues for changing the organizational structure to allow for this lie in the stories of those who've left and what they're doing now.

But first consider again Thuyet Nguyen, the 35-year-old Vietnamese refugee we met earlier. He said, "We're creating our own culture here, and it's something that is unique and beautiful." Like the refugee, the dechurched create thoughtful, diverse sets of practices that combine elements of their heritage and tradition, but in new contexts.

At the end of every interview we conducted for this project, we asked some key questions in order to understand what our respondents' lives look like now that they're done with church.

"How do your beliefs impact your daily life? How do you live out your faith outside of church? Can you imagine a church you'd come back to? What would that look like?" Their answers varied widely, but there were some common themes.

Some have left and aren't coming back. They're not willing to be reengaged. They can't even begin to imagine a church they'd like. Their histories are so filled with truly awful things that returning would be irrational and unhealthy. (In fact, as we were compiling their stories, Ashleigh created a list we called "Unbelievably Terrible Things" that cataloged the awful things our respondents saw and experienced at church.[1]) They aren't weaker Christians than those who stayed. They aren't less faithful. They aren't backsliders or spiritually immature. They have simply endured too much in the institutional church and see no reason, theologically or practically, to continue in that relationship.

Probably the best thing people in the church can do for them is to be open to hearing their stories without judgment or ulterior motives, hug them, and apologize.

But the message of this book is not that people have left the church and aren't coming back. The people who've left and cannot imagine a way back to organized religion comprise a relatively small group. Fewer than a dozen of our respondents were in this category.

Instead, the vast majority of our respondents were either actively looking for the right circumstances to reengage with a church, creating a new church paradigm themselves, or at least open to the idea that something could come along.

Perhaps most important, they were able to tell us what it would have taken to keep them engaged with their churches before they decided to leave. A lot of their answers sound very much like Chloe's:

---

[1] There's no need to bang people over the head with how awful the church has been at times. If you'd like empirical proof that our respondents who can't imagine returning to the church aren't spiritually weak or "baby Christians" (as one pastor labeled them), please do get in touch with me. I'm happy to share.

I'd like to be in a church that focuses on your value as a person and your value to the community as opposed to what you believe and who you are. I grew up with the idea of churches being about belief and a certainty about it. But I think churches should encourage rich relationships and thinking for yourself, and they should be open to changing their own thinking as they recognize that there are many ways to think that are equally valid as opposed to judging people. Am I looking for a church that "fits" my beliefs? No, not necessarily. I'm just looking more for a church that's accepting of everyone and accepting of questions. A church that recognizes that, you know, when a person says we're in different places spiritually, it doesn't create a hierarchy of people. It doesn't say, "OK, you're a baby Christian. I'm the senior pastor; I'm in leadership. You're just a congregant."

In the pages that follow, we'll dig into the version of church put forth by Chloe and so many like her to see if we can derive some strategies for churches interested in capturing some of the energy and devotion the dechurched offer. We'll pull together findings from preceding chapters to point out some unifying principles that could work to keep people engaged with church in the first place and reengage the dechurched in a way that will ultimately make for a more vibrant and impactful church.

FOUR STRATEGIES TO ENCOURAGE REENGAGEMENT

In the course of our interviews, we've uncovered four things churches can do to help the Dones reengage with organized religion without completely turning existing congregations upside down and driving away those who currently attend.

The key to all of these suggestions is moderation, and we'll explore them in detail in the pages that follow.

Invite participation—with limits. Identify key ways people can participate meaningfully with no barriers to entry. Give them some control over organizational resources, such as staff time and money, with little or no oversight. Trust your community.

Undermine bureaucracy. Put timelines on some positions and committees so that they dissolve when the timeline ends no matter how well or poorly things are going. Bureaucracy leads to unhealthy concentrations of power; this strategy helps to undo that.

Be truly relational. Devote staff time and resources to knowing and supporting people rather than creating and maintaining programs. Do things *with* congregants rather than *for* congregants. Offering programs leads to a service-provider mentality wherein congregants feel the staff exists to serve them. Being in relationship with people means supporting their work and doing things with them as partners. It means working on other people's ideas as if they were your own.

Impact your community…and be impacted. Be involved locally at the grassroots level. Need and unfairness are everywhere. Work to be a change agent. Churches often try to do this as mission work or outreach that "we" do for "them." Instead, allow the celebrations and struggles of your local community to change and shape your congregation.

Let's examine each of these strategies in detail.

INVITE PARTICIPATION—WITH LIMITS

Our respondents were excited about churches that earmarked some of their budget, staff, or space for projects or ideas that arose from within the congregation. This idea is actually founded on the organizational principle that work follows resources. In other words, if an organization creates space for work to happen, work will naturally occur to fill up that space. The challenge is to keep those resources set aside from normal, day-to-day operations.

If congregants sense that every dime is spoken for, every room booked, and all staff members constantly busy, they'll conclude there's no room for anyone else to do anything else. It's not that congregants will be unwilling to approach church staff with ideas; it's more the case that congregants won't have the ideas in the first place because they'll be getting the message that all of the work done in the organization is done by paid staff.

20 Percent Time

The principle that work follows resources has widespread adherence in the for-profit world, and we can learn by exploring some of them. Most famously, Google is known for its "20 Percent Time." One-fifth of each employee's workday is set aside to pursue special projects and passions within Google's overall mission and framework.

This idea relies on three fundamental organizational insights.

First, large bureaucracies can't possibly centralize true innovation. CEOs and other managers simply have too many responsibilities to be able to understand all of the facets of their industries. Twenty percent time intentionally structures in innovation.

Second, an organization that isn't failing often isn't succeeding ever. Of course, no organization intentionally sets out to fail, but failure has remarkable advantages. For churches, failure is an opportunity to learn, grow, and communicate to congregants that church leadership doesn't have all the answers and could use their help. It opens doors to new ideas and shakes organizations out of old routines. However, failure works best when it's structured and contained, when it's allowed to happen by design and doesn't spill over into all parts of the organization.

Third, the biggest asset of a truly strong and flourishing organization is its people, not a person. A church built around a person rather than its people is much more vulnerable than it might appear. Twenty percent time doesn't just communicate that people are valued and their ideas matter. It also diversifies an organization, incubating ideas and allowing people to exercise their talents while returning value back to the organization.

Ryan Tate said this about Google's policy in an article in Wired magazine: "Twenty percent time has always operated on a somewhat ad hoc basis, providing an outlet for the company's *brightest, most restless, and most persistent employees* —for people determined to see an idea through to completion, come hell or high water."[2] (Emphasis added.)

Sound familiar? The dechurched are precisely the same kind of bright, restless, persistent people who are determined to see an idea through to completion but are stymied by their organizations.

It's probably not realistic to devote a full one-fifth of a church's organizational resources to pet projects and wild ideas. But the data about the dechurched suggest that it makes sense to devote some organizational resources to provide an outlet for the church's most ambitious congregants. The percentage matters far less than the existence of the policy and implementation of the practice.

If you're a church leader, stop reading for just a moment and ask yourself, "What would it look like to set aside some of our resources for unprogrammed use or for emerging projects? What do we have at our disposal that we could offer congregants?"

Maybe it's a few hundred dollars a month from the church's budget. Maybe it's an underutilized room in your building. Maybe it's a staff member who seems to have extra time. What would the people in your

---

[2] Ryan Tate, "Google Couldn't Kill 20 Percent Time Even if It Wanted To," Wired magazine (August 21, 2013). Ryan Tate has written an entire book about this called *The 20% Doctrine: How Tinkering, Goofing Off, and Breaking the Rules at Work Drive Success in Business*. It's worth reading.

congregation do with a few hundred dollars, a room, or devoted staff time? Have you asked them?

It's important to note that the vast majority of these kinds of projects have short life spans. They die for a whole host of reasons, including lack of interest and because they simply weren't good ideas in practice. The key is to allow them to live and die on their own merits, without the constant pressure to prove their worth before they're given a chance to develop.

Many pastors and church leaders will understandably be nervous that their congregants will do things that go against church teachings or core beliefs. For-profit companies have similar concerns. An auto manufacturer wouldn't let its employees run off and start a publishing house, for example. Clearly, missions must be aligned.

At the same time, 20 percent time draws clear boundaries around how much of the organization's resources are devoted to these endeavors. If a church were to turn over its entire organization to serving the dechurched, it would likely have a very active congregation...of nine people. It would be a church of leaders without any followers.

This principle of inviting participation with limits allows both groups to coexist. It provides an outlet and some support for the congregation's natural leaders while retaining most of the organizational resources for the vast majority of congregants who aren't inclined to lead.

UNDERMINE BUREAUCRACY

I'm not suggesting that churches eliminate bureaucracy altogether. Hierarchy and bureaucracy can be powerful forces for mobilizing resources and organizing complex work that simply can't be done without that organizational structure.

What most of our respondents reacted against are bureaucracies that exist not to empower others but to feed their own existence. They've crossed the line from being empowering to being reproductive. By this I mean that at some point in the life of an organization, either at a certain size or after a period of time, bureaucracy tends to shift gears from empowering the people in it to producing only more and more bureaucracy. Committees beget subcommittees, and resources are allocated to activities that perpetuate the organization to the neglect of much else.

So what can be done? How can we address the Dones' frustrations while retaining the good and necessary parts of organizational structure that make it possible to operate a church of 50, 100, 1,000 or 10,000?

Exploding Deadlines—This simple strategy puts end dates on some programs or staff functions that would otherwise exist in perpetuity. From the outset, some of the work of the church is designed to be project-based, not program-based. When the project ends, the church moves on to something else.

The idea is that activity stops when the deadline arrives, no matter what. Decide beforehand how you will know when the project has ended, how many resources you'll devote to it, and how you'll celebrate your team's efforts when the project is finished. Resist the temptation to replicate or extend the project, regardless of how well it went.

The rationale is pretty straightforward. Positions, programs, and budgets are much easier to create than eliminate. Often organizations find themselves pouring resources into sustaining activity long after the activity has ceased to be meaningful or effective. These are what I call productive activities. They serve to produce and reproduce the organization, but they don't serve any real purpose beyond that.

This is the dynamic the people in our study were responding to when they argued that the church works only to serve its own needs. Assigning exploding deadlines to at least some projects communicates to congregants three important ideas.

First, it lets them know that they shouldn't expect church leaders to do everything. Churches don't exist solely to provide services to their congregants. At least part of the church's job is to empower people to do things on their own. If a project that people liked ended because of an exploding deadline, they should have all of the organizational support they need to get it going again on their own.

Please note that it's vital to communicate at the outset the conditions under which the program will end. When I describe the idea of exploding deadlines to church workers, they often say, "We could never do that. People hate change." But this isn't quite true. The prevailing research about stress and change indicates that what people actually dislike is change they didn't see coming and had no control over. Knowing at the outset how and when a church initiative will end diminishes and can even eliminate the stress that often accompanies change.

Second, exploding deadlines let people know there are ways for them to truly impact the life of the church. They don't have to deal with a series of committees or an ever-increasing infrastructure. Having at least one area that continually cycles the people in charge so that positions and resources don't become cemented allows the people who are frustrated with bureaucracy and hierarchy to gravitate to the less structured part of the organization without tearing apart the other, more structured, parts.

The result is that bureaucracy and hierarchy can continue to exist in all of the other parts of the church without driving away the people who are frustrated by them.

Addison gave us an example of how this might work in practice:

> I would be so nervous about going back to a church that was full of systems and programs. I lived in those churches for years, doing everything. Well, doing nothing, actually, because none of it really mattered except to keep the church doors open. I'm back now, though, because this place is a constant ball of energy. Things start and end here all the time.
>
> We just did this big movie production for VBS. I mean the kids did it all with the help of some parents. They wrote, directed, filmed, edited, did the lighting and the costumes—the whole nine yards. It was David and Goliath. Then there was a big premiere and an opening night at our church with a red carpet and everything. The kids were thrilled. I got all excited and said I wanted to help with next year's production, and I was told, "Yeah, well, that's not really how things work here. This was just a one-time thing. But don't worry; I'm sure there will be something else that will come up. Maybe you'll have an idea."
>
> I was really put off by that at first, because I come from a long line of getting things done in churches. I know how to make organizations hum, but then I realized all of the energy that had to go into that production, and it was all volunteer hours. There was virtually no church staff involved at all.
>
> Then I started to get *really* excited. I realized this place is different. I know it's a small thing, but just the fact that there was no attempt—none, zero—to try and build a booth here like Peter wanted to do and live in this good space was amazing.[3] It's like they knew what that would eventually lead to.
>
> Later I came to understand that people were only willing to devote so much time and energy to these projects because they knew ahead of time that they weren't committing indefinitely.

---

[3] Addison was referring to Peter's response to the Transfiguration in Mark 9:2-10.

It was just for a period of time. There was no sense that they were signing their lives away.

Obviously, the whole church can't run that way, but there's just this revolving door of projects that's always ongoing. It allows me to step in and out of things without feeling I'm somehow less dedicated when it's time for me to step back a little bit.

Judgment is a big part of the story of the dechurched, and that's why Addison's final comment is so important.

She explained that projects with predetermined ending dates actually encourage her to be more active because she doesn't dread the end. Before, she said, projects, programs, or activities dissolved for lack of funds, energy, or interest, and the people in charge felt shame, pressure, or judgment for allowing them to fail on their watch.

To avoid these feelings of judgment, people do all kinds of things to justify their programs, sometimes creating activity for the sake of activity and ultimately burning out as they take on more and more to prop up ministries or programs that have simply run their course. Exploding deadlines eliminate the need for that kind of justification. They empower people to take risks and allow the activity to stand on its own merits.

Finally, exploding deadlines keep the mission of the church front and center in the congregation's consciousness. New activities are nearly always evaluated in light of the church's mission, but ongoing activities are rarely subject to the same scrutiny.

Years ago, I was talking with a youth pastor who illustrated this point. He said he realized he had to leave organized religion when he was asked to run the mother-daughter banquet at his church:

I was at a church two miles from here for seven years, the church I grew up in. I was the young-adult pastor, and every year I would say, "Why are we doing a mother-daughter banquet? Why? Explain to me why we're doing this. How does it extend the mission of our church (which was pursuing Jesus' dream in the world); how does a mother-daughter banquet help us pursue Jesus' dream for the world?"

Well, here's the answer I got: "The women on the women's board would be so sad if we cancelled it. We've always had the mother-daughter banquet."

His point wasn't that the banquet should be cancelled. In fact, he loved the banquet and thought that rituals and traditions were vitally important for the church in contemporary culture. He even noted that one of that church's strengths was a good organizational structure that kept traditions alive. What he objected to was the fact that nobody understood why they did a mother-daughter banquet.

Forcing at least some of the church to keep renewing itself makes everyone a little more conscious of its overall goals and mission and guards against doing things simply because they've always been done.

Once again, I want to emphasize that it would be a disaster if all parts of an organization tried to run this way. Nothing would ever get done. It would be meeting after meeting after meeting. But drawing on solid research on organizational behavior, I do believe there's good reason to establish a slightly different structure that coexists with the existing organization. Because resources are finite, this might require some initial shifting around but not the wholesale destruction of the current infrastructure.

Making room for the dechurched and the people who may become dechurched doesn't mean neglecting the vast majority of people who are satisfied with current arrangements.

BE TRULY RELATIONAL

In 2012 Steve Corbett and Brian Fikkert released the book *When Helping Hurts*. One of the book's central messages is that, rather than doing things *for* the poor, we need to do things *with* the poor, because only the poor truly understand their own needs and capabilities.

Their findings underscore the idea that the power of relationship is much greater than the power of service. In Corbett and Fikkert's model, there's a role for service, but it's circumscribed. Service is necessary in times of great need or crisis, but it must shift quickly into relationship for truly lasting change to occur.

The Dones consistently said that they see a role for both service and relationship in the church. The problem, from their perspective, is that the church doesn't often move past the realm of service into relationship despite what the dechurched see as a core message from Jesus to live in solidarity with those in need.

Here's what Chloe had to say about this as she was talking about the relationship she wants her daughter to have with the church:

I wouldn't want her in the kind of churches I've grown up in. I would want her in a community, first of all, but one that's focused on outreach along with an understanding of people. I value respect for people, and it's reflected in allowing them to make their own decisions...I think overall community and service are the most important things. A sensitivity of spirit and compassion are some of the things I've noticed that are missing from the Christian church, but I've found an online community of people who've left the church. It's really good at embodying those things—better than the church was.

In an era when the church spends so much money and resources on outreach, it's striking that the institution is perceived as lacking "a sensitivity of spirit and compassion," but Chloe's sentiments were echoed by many of our respondents, and, if national statistics are any indication, there are many, many more who agree with her.

Providing services leads to a unique tension where there's never enough, even in times of abundance. If the role of the church is simply to centralize resources and then redistribute them to people in need, then no church will ever have enough resources. The more power, authority, and resources that flow into the church, the more the church is able to do its job of servicing people, both those in need and its own congregants. Over time what this inevitably means is that nearly all of the church's efforts are directed toward pursuing resources and concentrating the power to allocate those resources.

Mark made this observation during his interview:

The church is internally focused. It gives a token observance to social ministry, but usually it's in the form of some kind of activity that will keep those in need separate and apart from the church—things like clothing drives or throwing money at something. The best the church seems to be able to do with regard to missions is deciding what people need and doing things for or to them.

I find it undignified. It doesn't involve truly listening to people in need or interacting with them personally. I've found that dynamic even in the most well-intentioned missions like providing clothes or food for people. It tends to just keep the problem alive and

> keep the dynamic in place of the haves controlling the have-nots rather than interacting in relationship with them in the way Christ has called us to. And that's a big reason I'm done.

There's a balance to be struck here, for sure. Growing churches sometimes need to build parking lots. At the same time, there's danger in giving over the entirety or even the majority of the organization to the pursuit of growth through the justification of service. For one thing, this dynamic can lead church outsiders to view Christians as selfish, inward-looking people and the church as a kind of members-only country club. This perception has been confirmed time and again in national surveys and books based on personal observations. The empirical research presented here is even more evidence that churches are perceived to exist primarily to serve their own needs and desires.

Churches' response to this perception is, understandably, to tout the community service efforts they're engaged in. It's true that the church is a fundamental source of charity in our society, but when it moves beyond its four walls, it tends to do so on a one-way street. How, then, can the church continue to provide services but at the same time be in ongoing, caring relationships with those in need?

Asset-Based Community Development

The answer may lie in the principles of an approach to community development called Asset-Based Community Development (ABCD).[4] This approach to strengthening communities and neighborhoods focuses on identifying and leveraging the strengths that currently exist in a community rather than focusing on its deficits or problems.

Perhaps most usefully, this model has been characterized as moving people from "clients to citizens"[5] by focusing on people's gifts, skills, and abilities instead of trying to determine what the organization can do to solve their problems. Focusing on what's wrong and then providing services to correct problems creates provider/client relationships in which the people with the deficit wait until a group or agency with resources comes along to provide something that will fix the problem.

---

[4]For more information on Asset-Based Community Development, see John McKnight and Peter Block, *The Abundant Community* (Berrett-Koehler, 2012), and John P. Kretzmann and John L. McKnight, *Building Communities From the Inside Out* (ACTA Publications, 1993).

[5]Alison Mathie and Gordon Cunningham, "From Clients to Citizens: Asset-Based Community Development as a Strategy for Community-Driven Development" (Development in Practice, Vol. 13, No. 5, Nov., 2003), 474-486.

This runs both ways. Not only do people who are in need wait around for services from people with resources, but agencies and organizations with resources actually create a sense of need simply by supplying the resources. The very act can inadvertently communicate that people in need are incapable or inadequate. The Dones demonstrated to us time and again that they're capable, talented, and driven. They want the church to draw on their assets, not provide them with services.

The asset-based approach starts with a detailed inventory of the strengths of a community. In a church, this means taking the time to sit down with all of the congregants and asking them what they're good at, what they do in their free time, what gets them out of bed on Saturday mornings when they don't have to be at work.

For a detailed example of an inventory as well as specific strategies for implementing this approach in a congregation, I highly recommend Luther Snow's *The Power of Asset Mapping: How Your Congregation Can Act on Its Gifts*. This book demonstrates how to implement asset-based approaches that engage the Dones and the soon-to-be Dones without alienating the vast majority of congregants who still want the church to provide some fundamental programs and services typically associated with the church.

Of course, it's not enough to simply account for a congregation's assets, though there's great power in that simple act. Assets must be mobilized and utilized. If there's a commitment to discover assets, there must also be a commitment to collectively utilize those assets in order for the church to truly be shaped by the people who call it home.

In addition, allowing space in a church for the agenda to be driven by people's skills and talents means giving up some centralized organizational control.

The results of this process will, of course, look different in every congregation, but the results are often surprising. For example, some years ago I was charged with leading an asset inventory for a project in a large city. The project was aimed at preparing preschool children in a poor neighborhood for kindergarten. We worked closely with the congregations in the neighborhood to determine what assets they possessed that could strengthen the home and community life of the children.

While the survey revealed there was little formal education in the community, it also showed a large pocket of people in several congregations who were gifted, experienced, and well-trained gardeners. These people were finding space in the city to grow substantial amounts of food. Many of them had come from rural backgrounds, and some grew food out of necessity.

Tapping into their skills, we developed an entire curriculum around gardening that involved math, science, and reading. Congregational leaders worked together to coordinate the activity and provide space for the gardens.

Perhaps the most interesting discovery was that congregational leaders had no idea that these were skills that could be mobilized. Of course, they knew there were people in their congregations who gardened, but they didn't recognize this as an asset.

A telling postscript: When we had first approached the pastors about this project, their common response was that they didn't have any money to give but that the children in their congregations could sure use some help. By the time I left the project, pastors were reporting higher levels of congregational activity than ever, and several of the congregations were planning more asset mapping to reveal their next big projects.

They had made the transition from clients to citizens.

ABCD strategies have been used with great success in community and neighborhood development for the past 25 years. I think they have great potential for churches as well.

The ABCD approach is inherently relational. It isn't possible to do a true inventory of assets or begin to mobilize people around their assets unless people are in relationship with one another. Of course, all the dynamics that come with relationships are at work here as well. So the process may be time-consuming and messy with little measurable outcome in the short-run. However, the potential for long-term payoff is enormous.

Mobilizing people around assets not only changes the perception of a church to outsiders, but it lets congregants know they have value to the church beyond their nickels and noses. It creates a strong sense of identity through concrete relationships with people who share similar interests, values, and skills rather than an abstract, territorial identity around attendance at one church as opposed to another. Perhaps most important, the approach provides a structure to engage people who might be inclined to think they have no skills to offer in building the kingdom of heaven.

To make this work, church staff must take on the role of coordinator rather than creator. In this model, people aren't "plugged in" to an existing program; instead, they're supported with the full resources of the church to live out their callings. The result is a much more vibrant congregation in which people show up, not because they were cajoled by a volunteer coordinator, but because the things being done, the projects and programs being created, are *their* projects and programs, drawing on *their* unique talents and gifts.

Church refugees have told us again and again that they're fleeing because their assets aren't recognized or utilized. Worse, they often report that church leaders and church structure actually make it more difficult to put their assets to work than if they weren't in church at all. When combined with a heavy focus on growth, this leads many people to naturally think that their attendance and tithes matter, but their talents don't.

Jacob's experience is one example:

> I hadn't been to my home church, the one I grew up in, for 18 years. I got a call three years ago asking why I hadn't been putting money in the collection plate. I said, "Well, I don't live there anymore, so I don't go there."
>
> They said, "Well you're a member on the rolls, so you really shouldn't be going to another church until we release you."
>
> I was 18 years old when I quit going there to go to college, and they called me almost 20 years later. It was ridiculous. It just really turned me off. Who does that? And to say, "You haven't given us any money," not "How are you?" That did me in.

Jacob's story is extreme, but the theme of valuing money over people was common among our respondents. None of them told us they were tracked down and asked to come back because of their musical talents or ability to work with kids or even because they were missed.

The asset-based model shapes not only the church's understanding of the resources it can draw on from among its own congregants, but it also deepens its understanding of loss when people leave. It's not just that a person who once sat in a pew and contributed a few dollars each week has left. A whole package of passions, desires, and abilities has walked out the door.

IMPACT YOUR COMMUNITY...AND BE IMPACTED

The Dones care passionately about the world around them. They strongly want the church to be outward-looking and engaged in their local communities. Engagement for them means that they're open to helping shape their local communities and being shaped by them.

Mason's story exemplifies this. He told us that it was increasingly difficult for him to align what his church was doing with where it was located:

> Our church is surrounded by single-parent households whose kids go to a crummy school. In fact, it's the only reason we could afford this building, because it's in a low-income neighborhood. And yet we never talk in our sermons about what Jesus wants

for these people; we know nothing about how they interpret or understand the Gospels; we have no after-school programming here for them even though that's a huge need. It's like we're an island of relative affluence that can't be bothered with the problems of our neighbors. You know, I don't really care much if they sign on to our statement of beliefs. I want to know what they think about God, because that helps me to understand God better. I also want to do what I can to help show them the love of Christ. That relationship is just not happening right now, at least not in the way that I want it.

Mason went on to say that his church occasionally does things during the holidays or other occasions to assist local families, but it's a one-way relationship.

Some will hear Mason's call to be impacted by the community as a call to abdicate core values and beliefs. But what the dechurched want is to retain core values while also recognizing the context of the church's ministry.

MultiFrame Thinking and the Wisdom of Crowds

In *Reframing Organizations*, authors Lee Bolman and Terrence Deal argue for the virtues of what they call multiframe thinking along with a strong sense of organizational vision and values. They suggest that strong vision and values keep organizations rooted as they consider a problem or issue from different angles, or multiple frames. A solid grounding allows an organization to move outside of its default frame of thinking without worrying that it will get too far afield and lose sight of its mission. The problem is that actually executing this multiframe approach is extremely difficult.

At the same time, much research has surfaced in the last decade that affirms the value of collective decision-making. At the heart of this approach is the belief that the crowd has much more collected wisdom than any one individual in it.

The Dones affirm that there's much to be learned by combining the ideas of multiframe thinking and the wisdom of crowds in the context of a church that is trying to be responsive to its community without selling out its core values and beliefs.

A Siren Is a Siren, Is a Siren, Is a...

When I cover this topic in my classes at the University of Northern Colorado, I ask my students to take part in a simple exercise.

I ask them to close their eyes; then I play the sound of a police siren. Then, without consulting one another, they write down the first things that came to mind when they heard the sound. The responses are extremely varied. Students describe feelings of fear, pride, annoyance, and concern, to name a few. They recall stories of harassment, being helped by police officers, dreams of working in law enforcement, and stories of family members who do. They talk about how they hated living next to a police station when their own children were young because the sirens used to wake them up. They even tap into larger discourses about current events that involve the police on a statewide or national level.

The lesson for my students is that a group's overall understanding of an issue is deepened and expanded by hearing a multiplicity of perspectives. They come to realize that none of their thoughts, stories, or experiences is more or less true than another. Everyone's list is unique; no one lists everything that is mentioned by the group. In other words, they know more about the police as a collective than any one of them does as an individual. Furthermore, they don't gain a more complete and accurate understanding of police in contemporary society by coming to an agreement. Rather, they reach a better understanding by sharing their personal experiences.

In addition to deepening understanding, this approach helps people identify common goals. For example, no community perspective is going to get the police to stop using sirens, but an understanding of how disruptive sirens can be for families late at night can lead officers to take alternate routes when responding to calls or to delay their use of sirens.

It's important to note that the University of Northern Colorado is a middle-class university with a heavy focus on teaching and serving a diverse array of students, many of whom are first-generation college students. When I first tried this exercise as a graduate student at Vanderbilt University, it produced a much more homogenous set of responses. They weren't better or worse; they simply reflected the fact that the students' backgrounds and experiences were more similar than their counterparts at the University of Northern Colorado.

How to Listen as a Church

It would be interesting to replicate this exercise in a congregation. But instead of police sirens, it could be built around ideas of grace or sacrifice or another core value. Furthermore, it could be extremely useful to invite the people who live in and around the congregation to have a similar discussion around the idea of partnership or service or love with a goal of understanding rather than agreeing.

There are a number of forms that listening can take, but one of the most interesting approaches I've encountered came as I was writing this chapter.

We got an email from Alistair, who lives in the UK. Given that the focus of this project is the United States, we didn't interview him formally, but he described something that was too powerful not to share. After he left his church, he and a small group of people began meeting weekly for meals and discussion. After a while, they decided they wanted to do something together to help revitalize their neighborhood. The recent recession had taken quite a toll on the fabric of the community, and they wanted to "put into practice the things we thought Jesus was talking about in the Gospels."

At first, they sat around and tried to dream up things they could do, but then they realized they had no idea what the community wanted or needed or how their activities would be received. So they spent the next several months going door-to-door in their neighborhood, having discussions about Christianity and God and service and "everything you can imagine."

One result was that their small group grew, as they were joined by several people who were interested in what they were trying to do. More important, according to Alistair, "we learned things we never would have even considered. We heard all kinds of perspectives that we would not have otherwise encountered."

They are in the process now of trying to figure out how to put that perspective into action, but they all agree they have a better understanding of their community and of God now than they did a few short months ago. Alistair said, "These past few months have revealed more to me about Jesus' vision for the world than years of Bible study ever did. There's just a power in hearing from people and talking with them."

Alistair's story demonstrates that an openness to being impacted by the local community doesn't require churches to compromise their core values. It simply helps people recognize that a truer, more nearly complete picture of any situation emerges when many viewpoints are heard and respected.

A church interested in making room for the dechurched and the potentially dechurched might consider folding a lot more listening into traditional church programming. Remember, the dechurched passionately desire to be engaged with their local communities, and their first choice is to do that work through their churches. Including different perspectives about how to achieve your church's mission can be a vital component in preventing people from becoming dechurched and reengaging those who've already left.

CONCLUSION

The strategies suggested here aren't intended as a prescriptive set of boxes for church leaders to check in order to keep their most devoted members. Rather, they provide ways of understanding how to turn the general dissatisfactions of those who have left into some productive practices. If people are done with old ways of doing things, these practices will help usher in new ways of tackling problems. The church hasn't had it wrong all these years, but it might need to evolve a bit if it wants to keep people from leaving.

Again, I'm not at all suggesting that the old structures be abandoned altogether. The approaches we've described allow room for both.

Mark made this same point in his interview:

> The current church structure does serve a purpose. There are a lot of people who find value there. But from my perspective, it serves too narrow a purpose. It primarily serves the purpose of order and routine. The problem is that they've taken that order and routine and rigidity and liturgy and applied it to absolutely everything. It's like *everything* has become liturgy. It's *all* routine. And a lot of people need that, but there has to be room for me, too. I mean, shouldn't there also be room for me in the church?

CHAPTER 7: CHURCH FOR THE DECHURCHED

As we move toward the end of the book, it's instructive to return to thinking about the dechurched as refugees in order to understand what parts of their heritage they abandon and what parts they find so valuable and worth sustaining that they carry them on their journeys.

When people are forced to flee their homes, it's often with very little notice. Sometimes they can take only what they can grab, the bare necessities for survival. The things they grab say a lot about priorities. In 2011, photographer Brian Sokol released a project supported by the UN Refugee Agency titled "The Most Important Thing." It showed refugees in camps with the one thing they grabbed as they left. It's a striking series of photographs and reminds us of how thin the line of survival is for so many around the world. Many grabbed tools such as axes or knives, but others clung to photos, family jewelry, and children's drawings. All the objects connected them to home and were the foundation of their new lives in a new land.

What practices, objects, and beliefs do the dechurched grab as they leave, and how do they put them to use in their new situations? What ideas, concepts, and beliefs do they leave left behind?

REFRESHED BELIEF SYSTEMS

First, the dechurched take their belief in God with them when they leave, but that belief is substantially different from what it was when they were engaged with organized religion. There is a much stronger element of faith and trust in God as opposed to a certainty about their own beliefs and ideas about religion. Many of the Dones described this newer version of their faith as "freeing," as they abandoned the legalistic faith they said they found in church.

As a general rule, the dechurched are able to explore the boundaries and edges of their faith, trusting that God will bring them back or keep them on track if they stray too far from the truth or central message of Christianity. They share a reliance on God and trust that God is intimately involved in looking out for them. This stands in contrast to their church lives which were more typically marked by a reliance on people and trust in the institution of church to guide their spiritual lives.

While it might seem the dechurched developed this reliance after leaving the church, I don't think this is the case. In many ways, it was through the organizational dysfunction they experienced while in the church that their faith in God deepened. Because the church let them down repeatedly, they feel no need to adhere to its teachings or belief structures without question. God, on the other hand, has not let them down. They trust God. God isn't threatened by their questions. God isn't threatened by their wanderings or experiences with non-Christians or other faith traditions. This is why many of the dechurched said that their relationships with God are stronger since leaving the church than they ever have been. As one of our first interviewees told us, "I lost faith in religion, not in God."

Elizabeth made this distinction clear when she said, "There are a lot of us out here who really aren't walking away from Christianity or from Jesus. We're walking away from the system." And when a belief in God is the only thing they have to depend on for spiritual survival, that faith becomes a core part of who they are while organizational structures, hierarchy, and dogma tend to fall away. Those things are simply not seen as worth carrying with them on their journey.

COMMUNITY

The dechurched also cling to one another. They deeply desire to be part of a community. They find or create these communities wherever they are with whoever is around them. The data revealed a stunning variety of communities: online communities, neighborhood-block groups, small groups still associated with churches, dinner clubs, Bible studies, and numerous other kinds of groups that met regularly and had an underlying spiritual component.

Ella revealed the element common to all of these groups: "Really, I just want a sense of community and people who will work together to do something good." It's that simple. The dechurched consider community to be fundamental to the Christian experience. They want to express and act out their faith with others.

The concept of church in the general sense is viewed as so central to their religious understanding that they're willing to pursue it even at the risk of creating the kind of structures that caused them to leave the church in the first place.

MEANINGFUL ACTIVITY

Finally, when the dechurched leave, they take the need to remain active with them. We began this research fully expecting to find that people were leaving the church because the church was asking them to do too much. We expected to find a lot of overworked, stressed-out people opting out of leadership responsibilities so they could take a break. This could not be further from the truth. The dechurched are, as a general rule, leaving to do more, not less. The church isn't asking too much of people; it's asking the wrong things of them.

> The dechurched are leaving to do more, not less. The church isn't asking too much of people; it's asking the wrong things of them.

The Dones are done doing things they find to be unconnected with God. Even though a stated message of the church is to be active in the community, and Jesus commanded his followers to care for the poor, the sick, and the hungry, the dechurched have experienced church as an organization that cares primarily for itself and its own members. When the dechurched leave, they take their commitment to others and to living the life they think God wants them to live.

The idea that Christianity is a way of living that infuses all aspects of life is deeply appealing to the dechurched. They see their faith as the opposite of an overly individualized and self-obsessed world. They view Christianity as an antidote to a disconnected, individualized existence. When they leave the church, they take a commitment to others with them and put that commitment directly into practice.

When they leave organized religion, the dechurched place an active faith front and center in their lives as they resettle in a new world. It both recalls for them an ideal version of home and gives them hope for re-creating their heritage under the new circumstances they've chosen for themselves.

At the end of all our interviews, we asked people to close their eyes and imagine the kind of church that would lure them back. In most cases, they could actually imagine such a church, and those data fed the insights and conclusions we outlined in Chapter 6.

But here's the thing: They've stopped spending their time looking for the churches they described. Furthermore, they have no intention of listening to people who are seeking them out for the purpose of attracting them to their churches. They're so skeptical of organized religion that they aren't even inclined to go to church with close friends and family members.

Churches wanting to reengage the Dones should recognize that it will be difficult, if not impossible, to get them back to church as it's currently structured. But the church can go to them. They're doing things outside of the institutional church. The church can join them. It can support the work they're already doing. There's a real integrity in that position that the dechurched will respond to.

But this can't be done with a shadow mission in mind. Simply walking alongside the dechurched as they try to figure out life outside of the church can be powerful. If those inside the church are hurt, confused, and saddened when previously active and devoted members walk away, then they know exactly how the dechurched feel. They're saddened that church didn't work out for them, but they're rarely angry. They're open to doing things with churches and religious organizations, and they can be reengaged by churches through the work they're already doing.

And here's another thing: They need the church, and they know it. Organizations have real power to create and maintain coordinated activity over the long haul. Without the organization, activity is extremely difficult to sustain. Meeting in small groups over meals for discussion, as many of our respondents do, is great, but it's hard to do week after week, let alone month after month and year after year. Our respondents told us how difficult it is to create and sustain community and how they've resigned themselves to seasons of communal activity, letting groups come and go as people had time and felt the desire to get together. The times between these communal activities are dry spells that they try to move past. There's a real opportunity for churches to serve that need and offer support and coordination.

PREVENTING AN EXODUS

Given the difficulty of finding and reengaging the dechurched, churches are much better served by trying to keep people from leaving in the first place. This doesn't mean investing in more showy lights and sound systems, watering down the message, or pandering to individual theologies. No, again and again, our respondents said they left the church because it's set up to be self-sustaining rather than outward-looking and world-engaging. The cause was never the theology, the worship service, or an irrelevant message. Again, those are reasons people switch churches, not the reasons they leave church altogether. One of our respondents put this succinctly when she texted me, "community>theology b/c community=church=worship."

The life of the church is greatly improved by the retention and engagement of those who are on their way out the door. Frankly, there is no other organization or industry that spends so much time, energy, and money training people while doing so little to retain them. But we're not encouraging churches to prevent people from leaving simply to keep their pews and coffers filled. Rather, churches are better served by spending time and resources in preventing the exodus because in doing so, the church itself is transformed into a more vibrant and vital institution. It can be the home that the dechurched want and need while also helping to bring others closer to God. It just makes sense that all organizations are better off when their most creative, involved, and emotionally invested constituents are highly engaged, fulfilled, and satisfied.

THE DOMINO EFFECT

The ramifications of the data presented in this book seem clear. If the church continues to drive away its most devoted and active members, then the institution will be irrevocably altered and diminished.

In 2011, the Pew Research Center released a study titled "The Civic and Community Engagement of Religiously Active Americans" which showed that the people most likely to be actively involved in a religious or spiritual group are older and well-educated and have good incomes. In other words, these people have a significant amount of social, human, and political capital. They're people who get things done, boosting the energy level of the entire church. They're also the people most at risk of being done.

When they leave the church, they engage other dechurched people as well as those who might become dechurched. Additionally, the activities that the dechurched long to engage in—community building, meaningful ministry, conversations without judgment—enhance the reputation of the church among the Nones as well.

All of these factors point to opportunities for the church. First and foremost, the church can be the place that coordinates the community activity the dechurched long for.

The church can be the place that coordinates the community activity the dechurched long for.

David Hayward is a former pastor and current curator of The Naked Pastor website and blog. He also coordinates The Lasting Supper, an online community and discussion group where people support one another along their spiritual journeys. We reached out to David because several people in our study mentioned his website as a place they were finding some spiritual fulfillment since leaving church. At the end of our conversation he said:

> You know, the one thing our people do miss about the church is community. That's the greatest potential asset the church has. It's not the teaching; it's the ability to create and sustain community. But the church doesn't get that. Even for me, community is what I miss most.

In other words, churches still have a role to play, but it may not be the role they currently have in mind.

Our respondents told us, again and again, in countless ways, that churches who care about the dechurched should...

- create community by eliminating judgment through open conversation,

- increase meaningful activity by undermining bureaucracy and emphasizing relationships, and

- do meaningful ministry by engaging their local communities.

But it will take those inside the church to come up with strategies that work in their local communities. We've outlined some general approaches, but a one-size-fits-all set of solutions just doesn't exist. Solutions will come from thoughtful churchgoers and leaders who are dedicated to action and are not afraid to fail.

Refugees create new cultures in new lands. They bring fresh ideas and diversity to their new homes. The Dones can do the same. People who have left the church and those who are at risk of leaving can be the source of new life and a bridge to new and emerging cultures in their communities. They can be seen as courageous entrepreneurs willing to put their faith into action with or without the church. They had the guts to follow the call of God as they understood it even when it led them away from the safety and comfort that the institution provides. Following their lead could result in a rebirth of the centrality of the congregation to community life in America.

It's important to point out, however, that there is no neutral stance to take on this issue. People who are fed up with the organization, but not with God, are leaving and doing the work of the church right now, every day. Doing nothing will only result in an empty institution. As the dechurched leave, they become ambassadors of the church, for better or worse. Unlike others who leave religion and the church casually, by drifting away, the dechurched leave because they're convinced that the current structure doesn't facilitate spiritual and community action.

As we say throughout the book, they're leaving to do more, not less, and they're doing it within a broader and more diverse community. They aren't exhausted or burned out. They aren't retreating to small, like-minded groups.

In many respects, then, the Dones and the almost Dones are the strongest bridge to the Nones. They're the ones most likely to come into regular contact and be in community with those who have never been to church. What story are they going to tell about the church? Will they communicate a version of church that reaches out to engage people in conversation, community, and causes? Or will they tell a story of a church that exists primarily to perpetuate itself? Will the church be there with them when they encounter the Nones and others in their communities? Or will the church be standing on the sideline, admonishing them for leaving? Church leaders have an opportunity right now to shape that conversation and the future of the church.

The Dones and the almost Dones are the strongest bridge to the Nones.

Again, we don't think the rise of the Dones signals the end of the church in America. But we do think it's a potential turning point. If left unchecked, the Dones' migration away from the church will become part of the bigger story of the slow decline of the importance and significance of religion in America.

The church isn't going away. The long history of religion in America is one of adaptation above all else. The church will persist and move forward. But there is nothing that guarantees that the church must play a significant and influential role in society. So while the dechurched do not portend the death of religion or the institutional church, the response to the dechurched may very well impact the vitality of the church in the years to come.

ABOUT THE DECHURCHED PROJECT

The Dechurched Project began as an academic project in the fall of 2012. I (Josh) was between projects at the time, having just made the transition to the University of Northern Colorado, and Ashleigh Hope was a student in my Sociology of Religion course. This project was Ashleigh's initiation into the world of academic research, and she proved very adept in an incredibly short period of time. She has since amassed an impressive résumé for someone at her career stage.

Our division of labor clarified and reclarified throughout the project as Ashleigh moved through the stages from student assistant to full co-author. We shared the task of interviewing people and continue to collect data for this project even as this book goes to press. We both undertook the arduous task of transcribing interviews, with the help of some students at the University of Northern Colorado. Ashleigh completed the bulk of the technical analysis of the transcribed interviews in the summer of 2014, and I wrote the book throughout the summer and fall of 2014.

We both feel a tremendous sense of responsibility to our respondents. Many, many people have reached out to tell us painful and revealing stories of their experiences with the church. Although very few of our respondents were bitter or angry at the church, these conversations were not easy to have.

Very early on in the project, people told us two things that have made us, admittedly, protective of our respondents.

First, they thanked us for giving a name to what they'd experienced. They wrote to us to say that they'd felt alone and as if there was something wrong with them for not being able to fit into the church. Lilly, a 24-year-old social worker, told us, "Thanks for letting me know that I'm not alone. It's a difficult time for me, and sad. You have helped!"

There are many other examples of these sentiments. Daniel, the 50-year-old construction worker who had "done everything imaginable from children's ministry to singing on the worship team to leading prayer ministries" over a multi-decade career in the church, told us, "Having the opportunity to talk and be heard was very positive and in some intangible way provided another layer of healing for me that's hard to quantify or even express."

And there's Nathan, the retired pastor who contacted us at age 78 to say that he had looked back on his life and concluded he had spent it in an institution that he ultimately deemed not to be worth his time and efforts anymore, an institution that had turned its back on him, because he had come out as gay.

We've heard these stories and dozens like them. We've cried on many occasions. And each time, we've felt convicted to get this project out to as many people as possible to let them know they're not alone.

The other thing that people told us is that we're the holders of a special kind of knowledge. Amelia, a 40-year-old educator, told me after our interview, "You know, I don't think I've ever told that story from beginning to end. Thank you for listening. It was really good for me to get to do that."

A couple of weeks ago, we were reminded again of the power of listening. One of the last people interviewed for this project told us, "Thank you for listening to my story. Nobody has ever cared before. At least, nobody in the church has ever cared."

For these reasons we both feel a great responsibility to get these data right and to portray these people accurately, to do justice to their stories. In a way, we feel we're the keepers of the dechurched. There's no agency or body or organization that tracks them, reaches out to them, convenes them, or supports them. Instead it's a loose, informal network of people supporting each other...or not. In many ways, we've become a voice for the Dones as this project moves along, but the voice isn't ours; it's theirs. We're simply the ones who have assembled their stories and conveyed the collective knowledge contained in their experiences.

ABOUT THE AUTHORS

I (Josh) graduated from Texas Lutheran University in 2000 with a bachelor's degree in English. After a year building houses for AmeriCorps/Habitat for Humanity and another year traveling around while waiting for my wife to graduate, I began my doctorate work at Vanderbilt University, where I wrote my first book, *The Emerging Church: Religion at the Margins,* an organizational analysis of the emerging church movement. I'm now an assistant professor of sociology at the University of Northern Colorado, where I teach sociology of religion, social problems, and research methods, among other courses. I'm also the co-director of the Social Research Lab at UNC, where I conduct data collection and analysis projects for local and national partners.

Ashleigh Hope is in the process of obtaining her doctorate in sociology at Vanderbilt University, where she researches topics in the areas of religion, community, and health. She received her bachelor's degree in sociology from the University of Northern Colorado in 2014, and her previous research experience includes a nationwide congregational survey for the United Church of Christ. She's currently a member of a church in Nashville, Tennessee, and is interested in the various religious and life perspectives that exist inside and outside of the modern congregation.

A NOTE ABOUT ACADEMIA AND RELIGION

In this book, we don't shy away from the fact that we're scientists first. That means that our commitment in these pages is to our data, not to an agenda. We're responsible for describing our data as accurately as possible in a way that people can understand. That's the task of any good scientist. We aren't weighing in, explicitly or implicitly, on any political debates in the church about theology, worship style, leadership construction, or anything else. We have neither the desire nor the ability to judge whether individual people have made good, healthy, constructive choices in their lives and relationships with the church.

This stance isn't a cop-out. It's simply an explanation of the role of the scientist. We can suggest some things that research has shown to be helpful in other organizations, and we've pointed those out whenever possible. But only you can decide what, if anything, to do with the data presented here.

What this means for you, reading this book, is two things. First, this book is primarily descriptive, not prescriptive. We know that many of the books you come across include something like "The 10 Things You Can Do to Help Your Congregation Succeed" or "The 5 Long-Term Strategies That Will Grow Your Congregation," or something similar. As sociologists and academics, such prescriptive writing is not only outside of our expertise, but also counter to the project we propose here. Who are we to tell you what to do with your congregation? So the division of labor we propose is primarily one where we describe what is going on with the general trend of people making intentional decisions to disengage with organized religion and you, maybe with the help of some of the many resources produced by Group Publishing and others, decide what, if anything, should be done about it. This division is both practical and ideological. We don't think you'd be interested in listening to some sociologists tell you what God wants for your ministry, and we wouldn't feel professionally comfortable making such claims.

Second, our commitment to the data means that the findings described here are in no way tailored to make you feel good (or bad) about yourself or your church specifically or religion more generally. They're simply the conclusions that the data have led us to. Some of it will resonate with you. Some of it may sting. We simply ask that you read with an open mind so you can gain some insights that you might not have otherwise been exposed to.

Sociological thinking is not common. Instead, we think of the things that happen around us in very personal terms. *People* are not leaving the church; *Sally* left the church. But in reading this book, I hope you found that combining a bunch of Sallys in an attempt to understand the general forces behind the trend of intentional institutional disengagement can produce startling insights. Although it may be natural for pastors and church professionals to become defensive as they read some of these stories, we actually think data can produce the opposite effect. One of the things that should become clear throughout this book is that a trend of this magnitude goes far beyond any one person. It's not anybody's fault, and nobody is pointing the finger at you.

Finally, you should understand that this project existed as an academic endeavor long before we got in touch with Group Publishing about the idea of writing a book aimed primarily at practitioners, and it will continue as an academic project long after this book is completed.

Understanding all of this is important as you evaluate the evidence presented to you in this book. If you're like most of the people Group's publications reach, you're an informed, critical reader who probably brings a healthy amount of skepticism to anything you consume. You should approach this book no differently. In fact, given that Ashleigh and I are not church professionals, your skepticism might even be heightened. But it's important to us that you understand our positions and impulses behind writing this book.